UK Property Investment: *The Toxic Truth!*

The Reality of UK Property Investment...
Don't Invest in Another Buy-to-Let Property,
Until You've Read This Book.

Peter J How

Disclaimer

Although the author and publisher have made every effort to ensure that the information in this book was correct at the time of publication, the author and publisher do not assume and hereby disclaim any liability to any party for any loss, damage, or disruption, caused by errors or omissions, whether such errors or omissions result from negligence, accident, or any other cause.

You are strongly advised to take professional advice from a qualified financial advisor before taking any decisions of a financial nature. This will allow for the specifics of your situation to be understood and proposed actions either supported or modified. The same applies for any decisions regarding taxation for the same reasons, you are strongly advised to discuss your ideas and proposals with a qualified tax advisor before taking action. Again, this will allow for the specifics of your situation to be understood and proposed actions either supported or modified.

Copyright

ISBN: 978-0-9957928-3-8

First Edition Published in November 2020

Dedication

To the many silent 'soldiers' of the UK property investment world, who battle on despite frequent attacks from those to whom they have done no wrong.

May you enjoy the rewards of your work that you have fought so hard for, and may those by whom you are attacked at least respect you for your resilience.

I, for one, salute you.

About the Property Investing Series

The Property Investing Series offers concise information-packed guides for learning and future easy-reference and provides information on further resources for additional information.

The content of the books is based on the author's personal experience and knowledge of property investing mostly in England, together with contributions from other Property Experts' knowledge where appropriate. Very similar practices to those in England are also used in the rest of the UK, although there are sometimes slight variations in each particular country due to legislation, of which you will become aware, but the principles are the same.

When the author first started investing in property, there was not as much information available as there is today in the form of books, publications and property courses. Most of the information back then was from America, and he used this to work out how to successfully invest in property in the UK He was therefore more aware of the American financial and real-estate system than that of his own country and had to make the necessary adaptations for the differences.

This second book, in what will be a series of guides, can also serve as a model for general understanding by anyone, from any country, provided they then find out how such ideas relate to their particular country where they are investing in property. Usually, most of the principles are often the same, although there can be a few notable differences you will quickly become aware of. The first book, called All About Buy-to-Let Mortgages, covered in detail how to fully finance your property empire.

The contents page, chapters and headings in the books are structured for highlighting the key topics within each subject area. This should therefore give a framework for easy understanding and quick review, as well as helping with future reference.

For those wanting additional information, in each book, there are references to further resources and, where appropriate, the opportunity to obtain property investor ***insider knowledge***. Such knowledge is usually only made available at the often very expensive property training courses and academies.

HOW TO CONTACT THE AUTHOR

For anyone needing to contact me, the author, about this book then please use the email address contact@peterjhow.com

Due to my busy schedule, please allow 24 hours during the working week for a response to your email, although I will endeavour to answer quicker than this if at all possible.

The email address of contact@peterjhow.com is also the one to use for all media enquiries including TV, radio, and print.

If you would like to obtain copies of this book in bulk at a discount, perhaps to give away to your clients, colleagues or employees, then please indicate the number of copies that you think you will require and I will make an appropriate proposal to you.

I am also happy to receive any constructive comments and suggestions for future editions of the book, where this will make the information presented even better.

Of course, the amount of information included has to be carefully controlled to make sure that the subject matter is easily understandable, and not something that will confuse people. Please don't be disappointed if you make some positive suggestions, then later I decide that these are not suitable for inclusion in future editions of the book. I can assure you that I value all feedback and treat any improvement suggestions very seriously.

For those readers who are also property experts in their particular field, and would like to discuss a co-publishing deal with me, please send an outline of your expertise for consideration at the email address given above. I would be happy to consider any suggestions for possible inclusion as a subject in the Property Investing Series.

If this book does not put you off investing in UK Property, you should learn how to get the best financing available for your property investment programme.

Download your FREE book-summary of my first book All About Buy-to-Let Mortgages:

www.buy-to-let-mortgages.org.uk/bonus

To find out more about the additional information, products and services go to:

www.buy-to-let-mortgages.org.uk

CONTENTS

Preface

The first property investing book I wrote was *All About Buy-to-Let Mortgages*, which was published in June 2017 and released on Amazon. I did nothing else to market it because I wanted to get my book companion website completed before I did that. Well, the website development took on a story of its own and took a lot longer to complete than I thought it would.

During that time, the book was steadily selling on Amazon in gradually increasing numbers without any marketing effort on my part. The reviews, although few, were very good. I would, therefore, like to take this early opportunity to ask you to give this book a review when you have read it, as it seems very hard to get reviews without specifically asking.

Please therefore hold it in mind to make the effort to give me a review at the end of this book. It really will encourage me to write more books, as I will get more exposure as an author if you give me a review.

Anyway, I wrote my first book as an investor who learnt from many years of experience as to how to get the best out of mortgage finance, as well as getting the best from mortgage brokers. The book contains ways of creatively financing deals that may be broadly understood in principle, but not in the detail that the book goes into on clarifying exactly HOW to do it.

In this new book, I spill the beans on what it is likely to mean to your life to be a property investor, and particularly one investing in UK buy-to-let property. The book is focussed on the more difficult-to-handle side to property investment that is very seldom mentioned elsewhere.

I tried to be light with the book title at first, but it simply did not match the content. I then resolved to summarise the bad points of UK property investment simply as 'toxic'. This is very appropriate as the things mentioned are exactly what the toxicity of something does; it is something that kills, injures or impairs an organism. If we consider that our property investment activity is an 'organism' trying to grow and flourish, we have our perfect analogy.

I could have more blatantly given this book the more descriptive title of *101 Reasons NOT to Invest in UK Buy-to-Let Property*. However, I think that might have upset a lot of people who make a living from encouraging people to invest in property from selling them property courses. I did not want to upset them. I therefore also decided to write a sequel book to look at the positives that counteract the difficulties mentioned in this book to add balance. You are probably more familiar with those positive topics, especially if you have read books by others on property investment or attended property courses or events in the past.

I brainstormed the topics for both the book ideas at the same time, positives and negatives. For this book, I easily came up with an initial 100 topics, whereas on the positive side I struggled to come up with 50; all off the top of my head that is. Whilst this does not account for the influential weighting of each factor of course, understanding both sides is important. If you don't realise what the negatives are at the outset, it may be too late to hit the brakes when you get into high gear in your fledgling property investing career.

If you need to know more about the positives after reading this book, look out for the future sequel that I fully expect to write and will be aptly called ***UK Property Investment: The Antidote!***

I think that is an appropriate title as there are positives that are needed to enable you to shoulder the negatives I mention in this book. Whether the 'antidote' will be sufficient for the future is another matter, only time will tell as all UK governments seem hell-bent on making the UK property investment business as difficult as possible in recent years.

Be aware that a lot of the property books have an agenda to attract people into property investment, especially those books written by those who either sell property or property training courses. However, I have no such strong agenda and would like to add the caveat that you need to be of a personality and nature that can adapt to the change property investment will bring to your life.

In this book, I reveal the many repeating matters that have come into my life over the past 15 years of investing in UK property. If you are just starting with property investment, this book will act as a great crystal ball to look into the future of what awaits you. You can then be prepared and take action to reduce the effect that such negative matters can have on you. To be forewarned is to be forearmed, as the saying goes.

You may decide, however, that you do *not* want to get involved in property with the insight I give you here. That will mean you have saved yourself a lot of time and possibly a lot of money by making that decision. You can then go and spend that time and money on something else you might be more suited to. Don't be fooled, property investment is not for everyone.

If you have already started in property investment, I am sure you will be able to relate to what I am saying, as well as make note of some additional topics you were not aware of.

Note that this book is about *Residential* Property Investment and not Commercial Property, which is much different. However, most property investors prefer residential property so this will appeal to the wider audience.

I would like to point out that the information given is solely based on my personal experience; although I have no reason to believe that it is much different for other investors. I have been on property forums and Facebook groups, as well as having met investors at many different meetings, and I have no reason to believe the experience of many other investors is much different. I have also been a member of my local Landlord Association for well over a decade now and I commonly hear stories that would reinforce what I am saying in this book.

Finally, I would like to make a point concerning the predominant property type that I have invested in, which are the lower cost and higher-yielding type properties. These properties are *exactly* the kind of investment properties that many property courses encourage you to buy as an investor, although there is often no mention of the matters that I raise here, which quite clearly comes with the territory.

I really wish you luck avoiding the seriously problematic side of property investing, and maybe, with the information in this book, you can take action that will reduce your exposure to the potential issues mentioned. I cannot see that you can fully isolate yourself from this however, but the clues I give you should help you steer your way through your investing career without suffering from an unbearable amount of such challenges.

I have already said it is not for everyone. I can go further and let you know that sometimes I have heard of people having nervous breakdowns through investing in property. These are not people from distant places that could be an exaggeration, but people on my doorstep, investing in the very properties that I would have been to view at some time. I have probably even been viewing the very same properties at the same time as them.

The decisions you take and the way you react to the challenges that arise, together with the kind of person you are, will determine whether property investment brings an overall positive or negative contribution to your life. I really hope you manage things so you enjoy an overall positive experience. Fasten your seatbelt for an exhilarating, and sometimes dangerous, ride on your property investing journey. I sincerely hope you make it to the finishing line.

Introduction

This book is for those who want to

- Learn from someone with 15 years of experience in property investment.
- Understand how tenants can impact on your daily life.
- Be prepared to deal with those who wish to *profit from you* as an investor.
- Be informed about the little-publicised negatives of property investment.

It is also suitable for those who just want to know what it is really like to be a property investor in the UK, investing in buy-to-let properties.

I write this as someone who needed mortgage finance in order to invest in property. In fact, I had only £5,000 in the bank, which was not enough to start out in buy-to-let (BTL). However, by using mortgage money, I have been able to go on to buy over 40 properties in the last 15 years. This would have been more apart from the world financial crisis we had when mortgage lending availability, as a result, was reduced drastically for a period immediately afterwards.

All the money in these properties is mortgaged money, so I have learnt to use the UK mortgage finance system in quite an advanced way to achieve this. My book *All About Buy-to-Let Mortgages* covers how I achieved this and what I learnt along the way.

Now, in this book, I focus on the practicalities of Property Investment. If you are new to property investing, by carefully studying this book, you will soon be way ahead of those who are just going to learn by experience. In doing so, you will be much better prepared for what is awaiting you rather than just learning by experience, like I had to do.

Studying the contents of this book and gaining a good understanding of the challenges involved in buy-to-let property investment will pay off financially for you in the end. Just ***learning by doing*** in anything almost always turns out to be expensive. For sure, we learn from our mistakes, however, it is much better to learn from the knowledge of others who have gone before us and made mistakes and discoveries which they can share for our benefit.

It is also true to say that things have not stayed the same over the 15 years I have been investing in property, I have to say regrettably. However, in the property investment business, you have to keep adapting to the changes and keep in touch with the changes taking place. You can then adjust and adapt to the property investing climate at any particular time.

In the UK, we currently have many rules and regulations that give us certain challenges which other countries may not have to face, where we are disadvantaged compared to property investors in those other countries. However, we also have some facilities in buy-to-let finance which are not available in most other countries, and this is mostly to our advantage compared to other countries (I have covered all of this in my book *All About Buy-to-Let Mortgages*).

This book will equip you with the knowledge to work, either by yourself or with an investment partner, on getting the best property exposure to suit your personality and personal situation. This could easily save you a lot of pain compared to learning by experience alone.

Be aware, as already stated, there are many books readily available on property investment that only emphasise the positives of being involved in it. This could be misleading, if you are only expecting good things to happen.

There is, maybe unsurprisingly, very little information available about the challenges that property investors face. Of the information that can be found, often in the form of comments on social media, I have found these to be very selective in what they say and there are many gaps in the information.

I can understand that maybe those offering property training courses need to be careful about what they tell you. After all, they are in the market of selling their property courses that make them money, rather than selflessly preparing you for what you are considering entering into. However, if any such courses refer you to this book before you ‘jump in’, or if they share with you much of the information contained in this book, they will be giving you a very good service.

Maybe you are already involved in investing in property and considering expanding further. You still need to consider whether you are suited to what will follow.

Learning about the difficult challenges of buy-to-let property investment might not seem like the most exciting prospect, but it is essential for you to go into property with your eyes wide open.

The absolute worst time to learn about it is when you have committed to it and cannot change direction easily, without possibly incurring significant lost amounts of money as you exit. It could cost you dearly to change your mind and move out of property investment, when you run into some of the issues I highlight in this book.

This book will prepare you to get into buy-to-let property investment in the best frame of mind. Go ahead and set out your stall to study and profit from the information contained in this book. When you face the issues I mention, you will be well-prepared to tackle them head-on, and you will be glad you took the time to equip yourself for your journey ahead.

About the Author

I have worked in the manufacturing industry as an employee pretty much since leaving school. I say *pretty much* because my first year was spent on property… on the lowest rung of the ladder… cleaning windows (no pun intended!). That was my first business venture, where my friend and I would wake up around midday and then go to clean some windows. We did this for some extra cash after leaving school at 16 and watching our old school friends and our girlfriends (one each of course!) go to sixth form college.

I just wanted to start work. However, it was 1980 and it was at the beginning of a recession, therefore it was not the best time for someone to find a job. Especially having left school with only a solitary GCSE 'O' Level in English! Nevertheless, after about one year of trying to find a job by walking around the local industries, I managed to get set on as an apprentice electrician. I chose this as my work preference simply because an older cousin of mine was an electrician and it seemed quite technical and therefore interesting to me.

Anyway, we sold the window cleaning business for a few quid to some other aspiring souls and left for our full-time jobs. My friend got a job down a coalmine. Yes, this was before the Thatcher years, and yes, I was born and brought up in the North of England. Apart from inside the pub occasionally, I never really saw much of my friend after that because he worked a very complicated shift pattern down the mine.

But in the end, I wanted to be more than an electrician and went to the local college to study on day-release and night classes, doing engineering studies beyond what was required for me to complete my apprenticeship. This then led to me climbing back up the academic ladder, going away to University as a full-time student and even getting a First Class Honours Bachelor of Engineering Degree.

It was hard work. Although it just shows what you can do when you are interested in something and want to rise to a challenge. I took great pleasure in blowing away all those ex-sixth-formers at University as none of them got a First! It was just two others and me who got first-class honours degrees out of our studies. Interestingly, these other two people had also come the same route as me, by part-time study to get into University (OK, Polytechnic as it was then, but University as it is called now, and University sounds better anyway!).

Not to be defeated by thinking I could only get a top result at Polytechnic, I later enrolled on a Master's Degree course run by the University and came out on top again with a *Pass with Distinction*. I was the only one to get that I recall. I was then asked by the University if I would do a doctorate. However, that was to be the end of my academic studies for me as far as my appetite went (I mean... to go from Window Cleaner to Doctor?!). By then I had simply had enough studying and just wanted to go and do some work and try to make a difference in the big wide world!

Out in the professional working world, I did quite well by climbing up the corporate ladder and having, at one point, a Factory full of people I was responsible for as a Factory Manager. During the early years of my career I had spent some time doing technical training, this was on the use and maintenance of bespoke manufacturing equipment. It meant I had to write technical manuals as well as run the courses for the engineers and manufacturing staff. This led to me taking a course in Technical Authorship, where I gained a recognised qualification for this through the City & Guilds of London Institute.

I hope you will find that my training and experience in technical authorship helps me communicate some of the more involved content clearly and understandably. However, as is often quoted, "Everything should be made as simple as possible, but no simpler."

Anyway, after climbing up the corporate ladder I came unstuck with some organisational politics, conflicting with some people in high places. I slid down a snake, or that is how it felt if you can imagine a career as a game of snakes and ladders! However, I was offered an alternative employment position where I could be very creative and enjoy what I do and still do at the time of writing.

The new job role was much more sheltered from the politics that I had hated. I hated the fact that you had to support those above you, irrespective of whether you thought they were right or wrong. The problem for me was that I would simply not do that, so I guess I paid the price for it. That is fair enough - if that is how the senior corporate world works. It's not for me.

At some point about 15 years ago, I started to show an interest in the property market in the UK. In fact, I did look at this even before then, about 20 years ago. That would have been a much better time to have started in property investment. Property prices increased so much in those five years and even doubled in value in the area I was living. Anyway, we can only benefit from the time we decide to start in property and that determines our story.

Mine has been a story of learning by doing and then benefiting from property price increases, before suffering from the sudden drop in prices due to the financial crisis in 2008. Then seeing some benefit in low-interest rates, helping me to get the cash to support the properties, rather than relying on making money when I sold, which was my original intention.

As I said, I learnt by doing to start with, making lots of costly mistakes. Then I decided to attend some of those apparently expensive property courses. Well, they seemed expensive but quite cheap compared to the money I had lost from simply learning from experience. However, by the time I attended the courses I had learnt first-hand most of what they were teaching. Although you can always learn more and I am sure I got my money back and more, just from a few tips I picked up on the courses and applied to my investing.

Now, after 15 years of part-time property investment, whilst keeping up my day job, I have decided to write down what I have learnt in a series of books that I am calling The Property Investing Series. I continued to work simply because I quite enjoyed my day job, it was quite well paid and had a company car and other benefits… so quite hard to give up if you don't have to. However, with the advent of some of the changes that came to taxation, I chose to retire from my job as the taxation obligation of working and having property held in my own name became too onerous.

I now plan to make this property series writing initiative an up-to-date venture by providing further information that will be accessible from the internet. Additionally, making the reader interaction available on the internet for the specific subjects covered, where appropriate. This is therefore much more than just a book-writing venture, it's intended to be a property investment resource provision venture that should give you more benefits than if I simply just wrote and published books alone.

You might be wondering where I am, at the time of writing, in my part-time property investment world? Well, I have over 40 properties and each one is fully financed by bank or mortgage lender finance. This is often referred to as owning property with No Money Down (or No Money Left In, to be more precise).

I have experience in a wide range of tenant sectors as well as different property types (large and small terraced houses, semi-detached, leasehold flats, and detached houses with large gardens). Also, I have experience in various tenanting models, from single-family lets to houses in multiple occupation. And latterly serviced accommodation, which is quickly growing in popularity.

The estimated total value of my property portfolio is currently just over the ***three and a half million pounds*** mark, and I now have someone who works full-time to keep the properties ticking over with new tenants. This is mostly for tenanting the multi-let houses in which rooms in houses are let on an individual room tenancy basis. I then have other people who maintain the properties for me on a daily hands-on basis.

I am still active in the business, however. My main role is to initiate and supervise upgrades and changes to properties; making them better and more profitable. Another of my roles is to acquire further properties following my current investing strategy. Therefore, I am still actively involved in the running of my property portfolio and regularly attend courses in the property investment sector. These are courses typically run over a weekend, where I still manage to learn things from and apply to daily business on my return.

My author name, as you can see from the cover, is **PETER J HOW**. I wanted my name to mean something to you, something that will help you with your property investment journey. Therefore, think of my name this way… **P**roperty **E**xpert **T**eaching **E**veryone **R**esponsibly **J**ust **HOW** to invest in property.

You can work out my age from some facts mentioned before, this will test your basic maths ability; which you will need for property investing, but nothing any more complicated, fortunately.

I make that my aim to teach you to invest **Responsibly** by making you aware of both the upsides and the possible downsides to the property ventures you can get involved in.

I could have been much younger writing this if I had started in property at a more tender age. However, I like to think of our age-in-property because we can all start at different times in our life. What matters is our unique property journey and how we benchmark where we are in terms of how long we have been investing to see how well we are doing.

Even then, this is affected by our unique character, which in turn can determine such things as your level of risk-taking which can impact on how quickly our portfolio grows. The main thing is to get into the property investment game and stay in there. Don't make big mistakes like some have done and then gone bankrupt. Not many go bankrupt, but some do.

CHAPTER 1

Financial Risks

Scammers Abound

The very wealth you already have is put at risk by the scammers that abound in the world of property. Property has always attracted scammers because there is a lot of money involved in this sector of business, even in just a single property transaction. Of course, the scammers are looking to take your money from you for very little, if anything, in return. They think you must have access to significant amounts of money to be at least considering going into property investment, or are already in the property investment business.

The difficulty is that sometimes it's hard to tell who the scammers are, simply because scamming is their artform. They will come across as very professional and you will not be able to distinguish them from the real thing (a true property mentor, teacher, or agent) until it is too late. Once they have your money you will have a hell of a job to get it back. I have found a stark contrast in the ease of departing with my money and getting it back again. I have previously made significant mistakes this way in property, trusting people and taking them at face value.

When this happens, it can cost you more than just your money, think about the effect on your close relationships that will be affected as well. Most importantly your life partner, should you by lucky enough to have one and want one. In my case, I lost over £100,000 of money that was not even mine (it was remortgaged money). This was lost on deposits for property that was never delivered. The deposit money was for off-plan properties that looked great in brochures, not to mention the projected returns shown clearly in the supporting tables.

In this particular case, the land actually existed and there was a legal title to it by the off-plan selling company, only for this land to be sold on to someone else later before any property was delivered. In one other case, the construction work had started but never got any further than foundations and a little superstructure. I could even see the apartments I had reserved in the making, but these might well have never been started as far as my personal wealth was concerned; I took a huge hit.

Before you think it is just me who must be crazy to get involved in something like this, let me tell you I now personally know a lot of people in those very same developments. These people are 'normal' people who also went for the same dream as I saw in the same brochure, and were then sold to during the property inspection trip to see the land. Amongst them are doctors and lawyers and other professionals.

That was 15 years ago now and, despite many years of trying, many of us still don't have our money back yet; but it only took about 15 minutes to arrange and send the money. This is therefore a major risk area to a property investor because you have to take action and, if you get involved with a scammer, it is likely to set you back much worse than if you had done nothing. But you have to do something.

Therefore, when it comes to handing money over to those who will then take control of that money, be very careful about how you are able to get that money back if things go wrong. Or you might as well donate it to a great charity, the choice is yours.

Similar stories of people attending training courses and then paying for next-to worthless 'advanced training' and even property mentorships are commonplace. This is not to say these are all bad, but it is a real potential negative and a possible trap in property investment, especially when you are starting out and keen to get going.

Joint ventures would be another example area of where property scammers operate. In the same way, they take control of your money and you might as well have given it away. In nearly all cases, butter would not melt in their mouths. They will always give positive stories, or in fact anything, except the return of your money. Your only recourse will be to take legal action, but if they have operated inside a company you will probably find it is liquidated before you can get your funds back out.

Carrying out extensive due diligence is the only defence, but you will never be 100% certain while these scammers abound.

Paying the Mortgage Without Rental Income

You have to pay the mortgage when tenants don't pay rent on time, or when the property is empty and there is no rental income due. I often look at my spreadsheet of mortgage payments and I wish the same regularity would also apply to rental income as it does to my mortgage payments. That would be a dream world; the key to a profitable property rental business is achieving as close to that as possible, which is not easy.

You will therefore need another source of funds to cover any gaps. These gaps in rental income can last for some quite some time, in the case of a tenant that refuses to pay (or, on a few occasions, can't actually pay). It could take up to six months or even more to get your property back from a non-paying tenant. Add to that the property is likely to be returned in a poor condition when you get it back, so there are costs of doing the fix up work and covering the additional time until reletting can take place.

Sources of funds to bridge this gap can most painfully come from your after-tax money you earned yourself. A better way would be to have a small portfolio of properties that can fund the deficits in some income streams with ones that are in rent payment and generating positive cashflow. This then at least does not have to come from your own pocket and is still money that has not yet been taxed.

Interestingly, although mortgage lenders lend against the value of the rental income (as well as the value of the property), they like to see you have an alternative source of income. This is presumably to show you can pay them even when a tenant does not pay their rent to you. Even more interesting, is this required amount of income does not rise with increasing property ownership. There seems to be an expectation that a portfolio of properties will, to some extent, cover itself. This is in line with what I have stated above.

Clearly, if you did have a larger portfolio and ended up with a large proportion of tenants not paying, you may not have the income to pay the mortgage(s). In this situation you would have to sell or face repossession if you could not pay those mortgage(s) from other sources of income. I am not aware of this happening very often to this extent, but I am fully aware of the tendency of tenants to not pay their rent. Usually I have at least a few people who need chasing, or even taking to court, at any one time.

False Yield Figure Traps

Those selling investment properties to you can easily massage the figures to make their offerings look like a good investment. I have known this in the past when their figures are even backed by Registered Institute of Chartered Surveyors (RICS) valuations. In fact, I have fallen prey to this kind of deceit some time ago, when I was greedier than I was careful, back in the times of rapidly rising property prices.

The yield figure can be presented in a way that it looks like you are going to get a no-brainer, even some local estate agents use it. But if you don't fully understand rental yield figures, you can easily be deceived. You need to be aware of what yields are and be able to calculate these for yourself.

Even when you know how to calculate the figures for the two basic yield figures yourself (gross yield and net yield), you have to rely on the information you are using as the basis for the calculation. The most commonly abused base data for a false yield figure is the rental income used. Simply by increasing that figure above what is easily achievable, you can increase the yield figures and make the deal look more attractive.

As just stated, in the past I have had these figures even validated by a Registered Institute of Chartered Surveyors valuation, so don't put much credibility against that RICS badge, as many would have you believe you can. You also need to do your own investigation in addition, and get comparables of rents that are currently being achieved for similar properties. The temptation however is to use the figures you are given, especially if the person giving it to you can back it up with some references as to the source of the data.

If you do accept the rental income figure as given, you are taking a huge leap of faith in believing it is true. This is especially true if the person giving you the figure will financially benefit, if you take the deal. In any case, it is a risk you simply should not take, yet many do. I have also made this mistake in my early years of property investing. I made the mistake of totally trusting the RICS rental valuation figures. This information is given to you here so you can be aware of this trap and avoid the same mistakes that I made.

As far as the RICS valuation goes, I remember one rental valuation that stated the figure in the seller's information guide (this was from a discounted property club) was 'at the upper end of an acceptable range'. I think I even got the message at that, but because I wanted to have the property, I chose to ignore this vital warning sign. This can be another problem with believing yield figures. There can be a desire to believe the figures, rather than taking a cold and unemotional look at the financials of the deal.

The trap of a false or exaggerated yield, is one you may face many a time. Just make sure you don't fall prey to it and be more pessimistic than optimistic when assessing the deal. There will be many investors who took the optimistic route, only to suffer financially for many years to come as they have to supplement the rental income from their own pockets to pay their mortgage(s).

This is also known as losing money, and none of us want to do that. A false or exaggerated yield can be a wolf dressed in a sheep's clothing.

Property Prices Can Fall

Property values can go down as well as up, the long-term average maybe up, but what is 'long term'? This also depends on the area you are investing in as well as some are more exposed to a price drop than other areas, depending when you invest and where those properties are in the property price cycle.

Since 2004 I would say that property has increased very little in value if at all, especially if you take into account the increase in the cost of living. Even if you don't take that into account, some areas are still at similar levels as they were in 2004. We have to take into account the correction in 2008 to 2010 of course, when we had the financial crisis. Who knows what correction may be coming now we have just had the coronavirus pandemic.

Investing in property is a long game generally, unless you trade properties where you are buying and selling property in a short space of time. There might be a moment of bad timing and you buy when prices fall. This can be the same with any investment, just think of stocks and shares, silver or gold. Property is not as volatile as these markets, but it still has its ups and downs.

You will often hear that property doubles every seven to ten years on average, as we will discuss later. However, you should also know that past performance is no guarantee of future performance. I think mostly that investment for rapid capital gain expectation alone has long since ceased in the UK, and most investment purchases will be made based on rental income potential. Capital appreciation is then a bonus, albeit still expected in the longer term.

This is a much safer place to be, but will not prevent you from showing a reduced balance sheet in the event of a dip in the market. When this happens, you will just have to stomach it and hold out for the longer term when prices will increase again. If you are aware it can happen, you won't be as surprised when it actually does.

Buying the best deals possible will isolate you somewhat from a negative equity situation. Although it is wise to be aware that property prices can fall so you are emotionally and financially prepared for it, if it happens to you.

Exiting Property Investment

You can't exit the property business profitably very easily in the short term, although you can very easily enter into it. It is therefore worth thinking about whether it is really for you. What are your objectives? Are you emotionally connected in some way with property, or are you just looking to make money? If you just want to make money it is best to consider other forms of business as well, before getting into property.

If you have bought property using a mortgage, there will be significant costs gone into it which are best spread over the time of receiving rental income. If you exit early then there is a chance that you could at least lose the money you spent making the purchase and financing it. The reflection of true value will only have anything to do with what you did with the actual property, and not what it cost you to acquire it.

If you have bought a property that would be typical for an investor to buy to rent out, rather than a home-owner purchase, you may have already restricted your market. Your market will likely be investors who will not want to pay what might be a reasonable valuation for the property. Finding someone to buy from you at a price that would cover all your costs on exit might therefore be a challenge.

If you managed to go the distance and hang in there for many years, your exiting of property becomes more of a question of taxation. This is assuming that the many years have finally delivered an overall capital appreciation of course. Let us assume 30 years to be safe. This is a little longer than most mortgages last, but you can remortgage at any time on to another 25-year mortgage term (or similar) and exit when you are ready.

Taxation will be a complicated matter and of course your objective is to minimise what you have to hand over to the taxman. This then comes down to the business structure you are using to run your business through. You might in fact have several business structures in place. You will need to take advice on this matter as this will be particular to your investment situation and what you want to do with your property portfolio and when you want to sell.

The strategy I was taught many years ago was to 'never sell'. Instead, you just refinance as and when you can afford to with the equity in the properties. This however also needs tax advice so that you do not fall foul of anything in terms of your tax obligations. Passing your properties on to the next generation also then becomes a tax consideration in order to do that as tax efficiently as possible.

We often talk about 'exit strategies' for each property investment, but inheritance is the ultimate exit strategy to consider. If you have entered property in a considered way, it is hopefully a long time since your initial investment. If it is, you are likely to be very much in profit territory. Alternatively, if you are exiting early after realising the business is not for you, then you are likely to be looking at minimising your losses.

DWP & UC

The Department for Work and Pensions (DWP) manage the Universal Credit (UC) payments. If you already have housing benefit tenants, it is likely you will have to move to Universal Credit with your tenants at some point soon. If you take on new tenants that are already on housing benefit payments, you will probably be on UC from day one with them.

As distinct from when the local council managed their housing benefit payments, the DWP don't tell you when a tenant has left. The DWP will just quietly stop paying you the rent if you are taking rent payments direct from them after applying for this with the UC47 (an application for payments direct when the tenant falls into arrears on their rent payments). In special cases you might be paid direct form the DWP from day one, but that is the exception rather than the rule.

I used to get housing benefit letters about the rent payments being stopped from the local council which helped in managing the housing benefit tenancies. I could contact the tenant to try to address the issue before the next payment was due, or at least get onto it as soon as possible. Since going to universal credit with such tenancies, I still expected some notification of payment problems, but nothing came through.

It seems that with UC it is fully on me to manage this income stream in its entirety, therefore I will now always have to be responding to late payments. We have lost the chance to be proactive and keep payments on track, by no longer getting the prior notification as it was with the local council housing benefit payments. The DWP also seem somewhat of a faceless organisation in that you don't get the same people answering the phone like used to happen with the local council.

Communicating with the DWP about UC also seems somewhat slower than when local councils managed the housing benefit payment. It is now mostly done by email, although they will call you if something needs to be discussed. I have found some of the staff quite helpful, but the system you have to work with is quite cumbersome and slow, which makes letting to housing benefit tenants much harder than it used to be.

It is even frustrating for the housing departments in the local councils as they can no longer find out what is happening with payments. They used to use that information to try to help housing benefit tenants, as well as helping landlords rightly get their rent payments.

The introduction of UC has been painfully slow but that is probably a blessing in disguise. It is the brainchild of Iain Duncan Smith and fiercely defended by the Tory Government, despite it clearly creating more problems than it has solved. The whole idea behind it is to make the more vulnerable of society fiscally responsible... can you believe that? The people that come up with these ideas have not lived in the real world, at least not the world of property lettings that I live in.

However, the drugs market will have seen a boost in its income after the introduction of UC with payments going to tenants. Of course, not all this money is channelled that way, but you can expect an appreciable amount will go on recreational aspects of a tenant's life. At least as landlords we have the safety net of the UC47 form, as long as you have the required information about your tenants to fill it in fully, which hopefully you will have, including tenants' dates of birth and their national insurance numbers.

No More Arrears Payments

Still on the topic of DSS payments, as we often still know them as, there has been a change where anything more than one-month owing does not get paid to you. In the past you would get this if there was just some administration error that caused the stoppage. I have had corrections in rent payment of up to 4 months in the past, which amounts to a lot of rent money.

Instead, the new approach is to pay just the one-month arrears and you lose the rest when the local council is paying. With Universal Credit, you might get similar treatment but in addition you will be able to claim an additional deduction from their payment going forwards. This assumes you apply for the additional payments available when submitting the UC47 form.

The additional payments made under the UC47 will be paid at a fraction of the amount of the monthly rent amount, so it will take quite a long time to get back several months of rent arrears.

There is an issue we now have with the gradual repayment of the rent arrears under UC47, however. That is the fact that if the tenant moves out of your house, you will no longer get these arrears payments. This can of course be an incentive for the tenant to leave in order to cancel their debt payment to you and take the money for themselves again.

However, it was good for landlords to get this additional payment option, but a shame it cuts off and allows tenants to walk away from their financial responsibility, especially when it is supposed to be all about teaching them fiscally responsibility. Something is not quite right there.

Despite all of this, you could say that it is the tenant who still owes the money. That is true, but it would be difficult to get the payments from them if it cannot be taken directly from their benefit payment. There is often not really much money left for them to pay with, even if they wanted to, although many don't even want to pay regardless. It used to make me laugh when there was a letter from the council about the benefit being stopped for some reason, then there being a sentence telling you to recover the full rent amount direct from the tenant… as if.

Less Hassle, Less Money

Property investment is not really the passive investment it is made out to be, as we will cover in more detail later. It turns out that the more passive your investment is then the less money you are likely to be making. This is a general rule, but one I would stand by.

I can justify this in a few ways. Let us take the example of the best payers there are as tenants. These are the professional people that have something to lose if they have anything adversely affect their credit rating, such as a non-payment of rent could lead to, if you put a money claim in on them as their landlord.

These professional type tenants tend to prefer higher value properties and as a general rule these then tend to be lower-yielding, so you don't make as much income as a percentage of the cost of the property. To make these properties work from a cashflow point of view, you will typically need to have more deposit left in the deal to keep the financing costs low enough to leave headroom for profit.

This means you get less money out for the money invested, although it is likely to be less hassle because this tenant type will more likely behave themselves and pay the rent regularly. It would be very hard to make this type of property cashflow when taking out all your invested money back out after refinancing later, which is the aim of most investors, as it generates so-called infinite return on investment. You might have to wait for many years of rent increases before you can actually do this.

At the other end of the spectrum, you can have low-priced housing such as terraced houses in social housing areas. These properties will give you a very high yield and more easily allow you to extract any invested capital. This of course assumes you bought at a good price and then added value to the property before refinancing. In this case, the amount of rent achievable can often easily support a refinance to the elevated capital value. (This is all explained in detail in my book *All About Buy-to-Let Mortgages*, if you are interested in knowing more about how to do this exactly.)

However, as you will have gathered from the discussions so far, this kind of tenancy is more likely to need some active involvement in managing social behaviour and ensuring continuity of rental income. There are of course a range of investment options in between these two extremes, but I give these examples to illustrate the general rule I stated.

It also applies to Houses in Multiple Occupation (HMOs) and Serviced Accommodation (SA) which needs more work input. (The average income of the tenants would also have a notable effect on these kinds of accommodation too in their own right, similar to that described above.) HMOs have more challenges to deal with in terms of potentially higher turnover of tenancies and managing relationships inside the houses. SA needs cleaners and more regular maintenance and often needs a team of people to support these activities.

If you can systemise this, or outsource it effectively, you might isolate yourself somewhat from the hassle but it will still be there to be dealt with by someone. This will come at an additional cost to running your operation. The fact remains that you need to put in the work to get more back from your money invested. Or put another way: the more money you expect to make, the more hassle you will have to deal with, in one way or another.

Interest Rates Can Rise Suddenly

It might seem hard to imagine, for many people, that interest rates could rise sharply. This would in fact destroy the investing model of most people in the modern property investment world. Of course, for those with fixed mortgage deals then there would be protection from this during their fixed-interest period. For those with variable-rate mortgages, the hit would be sudden and quite drastic. In a sense, we are gambling on interest rates staying low when we are on a variable-rate interest mortgage. I have many of these mortgages, but also some fixed rate mortgages as a hedge.

In 2007 the base rate was at 5.5% and this made most standard variable rate mortgages around 7.5%. This fell drastically in 2008 when the financial crisis struck and since then it has never returned to such higher rates. However, the long-term average of the Bank of England base rate is about 5%. We are now in an unprecedented low interest-rate environment and it is probably something that many investors have never known to be any different.

Shocks to the world and its economy however are clearly something we might now come to anticipate. Fortunately for investors, when the economy is not doing very well, there is tendency for the interest rates to be set low. However, the main tool that is used to help control inflation is the Bank of England base-rate of interest. This means if something initiated a sudden increase in inflation, interest rates would very likely have to be increased to control it.

I remember when I first started investing, I was meeting people who were reminding me that interest rates only a few decades earlier or so had been at 15%, in an effort to control rising inflation. This led to a lot of property repossessions at that time and people struggling to keep hold of their homes.

There were many people buying properties for investment even back then, and those I knew had to exit the market as they had just used finance to help make their purchases in some way. This was at a time before buy-to-let mortgages were available and so commercial finance had to be used. This would include the additional pressure of paying back the capital and doing so over a shorter period than is often associated with a typical mortgage term.

A sudden increase in interest rates is therefore something that could happen again, even though I can't imagine the circumstances upon which a sudden increase in rates would be triggered. However, we have had events recently that has put the world into lockdown that we also could not have imagined just six months prior. Things can change quickly and uncontrollably.

Borrowing money to buy investment properties therefore carries the risk of an increase in cost that you cannot be fully in control of. It could be a threat to your investment empire you may have built up over the years. This might be very unlikely, but at the same time, entirely possible.

Expensive Property Problems

Property can have some difficult problems that are expensive or difficult to solve. You may well only find out about this after you have bought a property and find something that was not found by a survey, assuming you actually had a survey done. (If you are buying with cash of your own rather than a mortgage, surveys are optional, albeit still recommended. Where you buy with a mortgage there will be a survey done on behalf of the mortgage company, although this will not be an extensive survey.)

Properties can have structural problems that might not be evident to a mortgage valuation survey. You would need a full structural survey in order to be fairly sure there are no such issues before you buy. This is not normally done due to the expense of these surveys and the fact that it is rare to come across such issues that are not evident with a standard home buyers survey. However, it is possible, and if you are buying many properties there is a good chance you will be affected by a structural issue at some point.

It won't be possible to look for help from the mortgage company, in fact they will be using you as an effective layer of insurance in order to not require a more thorough survey. That is, the legal owner of the property will have to sort out any serious problems before selling later, if such a problem comes to light.

If you did have to sell with a problem, and get a lower price for the property because of it, you would still have the liability to pay the mortgage company for any shortfall at the time of the sale. In this way, the mortgage company can take somewhat of a risk with a very basic survey and then rely on any subsequently found serious problems being sorted out by the landlord.

The expense of such a fix-up is not going to increase the value of the property and is therefore an out-and-out cost. This assumes the property was sold without any account of the problem of course, and therefore not reflected in the purchase price. In some cases, properties may need such expensive things as underpinning to provide better foundations to an existing building. Roofs could also be a structural liability and in fact walls may not be straight and need taking down and rebuilding.

All of these are easy to miss on a cursory valuation survey, and possibly on a Homebuyer's Survey, if slight in nature at the time of the survey. You therefore have this risk you take on when you buy a property, even having had a survey done.

Auction Property Is Very Risky

I know the TV presenters make this look very glamorous and exciting, however the reality is that buying property at auction is very risky. I can give you my experience to help illustrate the point on several key areas of concern.

The brochures that you get will show the best features of the property. The price of the property might seem very low and you could not have anything to lose, that is if there isn't any bidding war in the auction room about it. The temptation could be even to bid blind without even having been to see the property. This could be a very serious mistake in some cases.

I remember seeing a property in an auction which showed it as a terraced house on a small terraced row. The location was not too far from me so I decided to take a look at it. I was somewhat shocked to find that it was totally burnt out and the rear of the property had collapsed although from the roadside it looked like a complete property, as per the auction details.

I can imagine the shock of the person buying that house. It would not have been an asset they had just committed to buy, but a liability. I dread to think, and it would not be nice thoughts if I did. Also, in the local area there had been a programme of demolishing the houses nearby to 'clean up' the area.

This small terraced row was at the side of the demolition site so may have fallen just outside of the demolition programme. However, someone had seen fit to make it join the ranks of the other demolished buildings, by setting fire to it. I am not sure to this day whether it was actually placed in the auction that way, or whether the damage was done after the auction details were publicised. Irrespective, the result of a winning bid for someone would have been the same.

In peak market times, when auction houses are very popular places, I have seen bids for even very sound properties go well above what the normal market price should be. I went to one auction with a view to making a purchase of a property that was on the same street as another property I had recently purchased. I had done the viewing and worked out what I would do to it to add good value. Everything was in order to allow a refinance soon afterwards and get all my money back out of the deal, as long as I got it for the right price.

I knew the end value of the property after the work I was going to do to it and from that I worked out what I would be willing to pay for it. I registered at the auction and got my bidding number and waited for the lot to arrive for bidding. To my amazement, the bids immediately started coming thick and fast. I raised my number to join in the bids, but before I had lowered it again, another number had gone up. I put it up again and the same thing happened.

I realised this was a race that was going to drive the price way high so I just laughed at my misfortune in trying to chase this one to auction, and simply watched the bidding take place. The final bid was in fact very near to the final valuation I would have put on the property after a significant refurbishment and remodelling. Therefore, although the buyer would actually be getting a good house they were going to be able to work on and rent out, unlike my first example above, they were going to be in negative equity from point of purchase.

The amazing thing was there were plenty of others who were bidding it up and took it way out of its real value range. This was in the times when property prices were increasing quickly. I therefore think some emotions were running high and that was coupled with people who were probably new to property investment and/or not knowledgeable enough about the local house prices. It was an expensive mistake to make, but at least they got a house.

Once you have committed to a purchase under auction conditions, you have to go through with the purchase. If you don't you will at least lose your deposit payment which is typically 10% of the sale price plus action fees added. If you did decide to back out then you may also be chased for the difference in what you offered against what it finally sold for. This could be substantially less than what you offered.

Because of this, some will say you should have a survey done on any property that you are going to bid on in auction. Whilst this is a very safe option to suggest, valuations are not very cheap and could therefore it could easily be a waste of money if you are bid out of the room, just as in the example I gave above.

It therefore remains a risky area in buying property. However, as with most things, where there is higher risk there is higher rewards. I would suggest though that you leave this aspect of buying property until you are comfortable with what to look for and what the property values really should be. Even so, it remains a significant risk on many fronts.

Ineffective Money Claim System

Rent being owed by tenants is likely to be an issue to you, unless you are renting solely to professional working type tenants. Professional working tenants are very protective of their credit rating and are likely to ensure you are paid on time for your rent. If you can manage to provide housing that gives a good yield to this kind of tenant, you are generally in a good position as regards being paid your rent.

If you are renting to social security claimants or sometimes working people who are in and out of work as a lifestyle, you are likely to have rent arrears at some point. The level of arrears will depend a lot on how you manage it, but the fact is you will be owed money. This is a fact of renting and a battle you will have to face at some point, even if you are lucky enough for it not to be a regular occurrence.

In dealing with getting the rent money owed to you, you will of course have to try to deal with it by direct communication with the tenant to remind them to pay. You can then escalate this with a demand for payment by a certain date. You can next threaten eviction if no payment is made leading to the issuing of a Notice to Quit. If still no payment is made, it can take on a life of its own that may lead to court action being taken and finally a bailiff to enforce the eviction.

Outside of this, you have other options to get your money, albeit these options are not as effective as these should be to protect landlords. However, as we discuss elsewhere, protection of landlords' income is not something that is on the agenda of those who make and pass the housing laws we have to deal with.

One option you will have is to call in a private debt collector who can then take on the case. You can also submit the case to a solicitor who can write them letters and threaten the action of eviction at further cost. In my experience, the private debt-collectors action is largely ineffective and I would be very careful who you set on to do this for you.

Solicitors serving notices is not something I can comment on as I have not done this due to costs for sending letters out and the likelihood of response from the tenant types I have. However, if you can find a solicitor who will do this for you at reasonable cost, this could be an option. Even if it is an empty threat in that you would not go ahead with the action through the solicitor, it might still have the desired effect.

There are also private organisations focussed on debt recovery from tenants and who will also take it all the way through to eviction. In these cases, you should expect to pay handsomely for their services, which will add to your out-of-pocket situation. But you may get lucky and get some money from the tenant if they use their powers of persuasion carefully enough. This is a rare event, but it can happen.

There is another option that used to be very effective and I have used it many times in the past. This was a 'money claim online', and if you google that phrase you can get all of the details. I have used it to good effect in the past after discussions to obtain the rent money failed. I have also had county court judgements awarded solely by using this approach.

However, in recent years I have found out that it is more difficult to implement in that you have to provide a very good record of all the attempts to claim the money before you make the claim. You will need to show detailed records of what you have done and the judge will have to be happy that nothing else could be done. This was not so onerous in the past, and it is a shame that it has now got to this difficult-to-enforce level.

When you go to court with a Section 8 Notice to Quit, you will get an award of the rent arrears on the judgement if you are successful with your case. This is a County Court Judgement (CCJ) that will be recorded against the tenant. You won't be able to claim all the costs involved in taking the matter to court, but there are some costs that will be awarded on top of the rent owing.

Whichever claim route you go down, once you have the court order, you need to implement it and that is an entirely different story and not an easy matter to force payment. It might be that the tenant or ex-tenant will pay you to remove the CCJ from their credit file, although in my experience this is often not the case. It will expire after six years anyway, but in the meantime, they will have to deal with any credit searches that show this debt up on record.

All in all, you can see that claiming the money that you are owed is not easy if a tenant decides to not pay their rent to you.

Your Property Value Can Easily Go Down

One thing I don't hear mentioned very much is the cost required just to keep your property at a lettable standard. It is hard to put a figure on this as it will depend on the type of property, tenant types and the areas you have your properties in. Generally, the more upmarket you go the less damage you will suffer, although a higher standard is expected and that can be costly to maintain too.

Certainly, my experience at the higher-yielding single-let end of the market is that these costs can be significant. However, the thing is, that if you do not do the maintenance and refurbishment work required, the value of your property can easily go down. The impact of the appearance of a property can affect its perceived value greatly. Just as much as when you buy a property you can add value to it by doing the refurbishment work, a tenant's lifestyle in your house can easily bring the value down, then you have it all to do again.

I have rarely known properties come back to me in a better condition than when I let them out. I could probably count on the fingers of one hand when this has happened. I take this as a very welcome bonus when it happens. Normally the best I can hope for is fair wear and tear level of degrading of the property. Seldom do I get just this and I would describe most as significant wear and tear with a little damage thrown in for good measure.

It is therefore easy to see the value of your property go down unless you are willing to keep feeding it with money to keep the value as it was when you bought it, or how it was after you remodelled and refurbished it. I had a recent example of a larger house where the value had reduced by one hundred thousand, in the opinion of a valuer.

I had previously refurbished and remortaged this particular property about only six years prior. Basic levels of maintenance had been carried out and there had been numerous 'clean-ups' done over the years. It would have had quite some wear and tear as it was a house in multiple occupation, however it had not had a major makeover since the original one.

I then went for a remortgage to refinance to a better interest rate, but was then given this much lower valuation than the original one. Therefore, the value of my property had dived significantly, at least in the eyes of the valuer. That might be quite an extreme case, but I wanted to inform you of that to show you what can happen in the real investing world.

I could of course have put more work into it before refinancing, but I just did this as an opportunity since the valuation was free and I still expected it would have held reasonable value. If I was more desperate to get a remortgage approved, I would have been willing to put in a little more money to get the property looking back to the standard it was at six years ago.

This devaluation by the surveyor is not a major concern to me as I bought the house to get planning permission on the land that came with it, so please don't shed any tears for me. But I thought the significant lowering of the valuation figure was appropriate enough to support the point I am making.

Tenants Leaving Debt Behind

As previously discussed, the largest problem a landlord will have is with some tenants who do not pay their rent. The best thing that can be done when the rent is owing is to chase it up immediately and let the tenant know that you are aware the rent is late, and that it should be paid as soon as possible. Starting off with a nice reminder and then getting stronger on each subsequent communication.

There are some tenants who manage to come up with excuse after excuse. They can be very clever with starting catching up but then starting to fall behind again, slowly but surely. Before you know it, they are owing you quite a lot of money. At this stage, things get much more serious and stressful, maybe more stressful for you than the tenant who could be living like this as a lifestyle. They will however continue to fund themselves with such things as their car and other personal things, all with the rent money they have not paid you.

At a certain stage you might start legal action, which is another cost to you that adds to the amount the tenant is effectively costing you. How long they stay will depend on many things including how you handle the situation as well as their character (or should I say cheek?). What is for sure is that it is very likely these kinds of tenants will walk away from you and leave the debt behind them, only to start again with a new landlord.

I have found that despite the fact that they should come to you asking for you to give them a landlord reference, they will still manage to find another landlord without needing one. I am not sure how they manage this, but this is clearly an important part of the lifestyle they lead. Some landlords might not take the references they should take or maybe they manage to get a friend to give the reference rather than it being the ex-landlord as they make out. I can only imagine the solutions they can come up with for this.

The time and trouble in chasing this debt is likely to mean it will go with them, never to get repaid. This can be different if you manage to get an award by a CCJ for the money, but you then have to enforce that, which is not an easy process.

I can't remember the figure for the amount of money that is estimated to be owed to UK landlords in a year, but I know it was a staggering figure. All this money is being spent on other lifestyle choices, and maybe you can imagine what some of those could be (clue: probably not constructive to society as a whole). In most cases there is no real reason for not being able to pay, only not wanting to pay. Of course, there will be a few genuine situations, although I cannot recall many of those over the years.

I would say that tenants leaving you debt will also leave you with a few other issues to deal with, not least of which will be the condition of the property. It seems to go hand-in-hand with poor-paying tenants who walk away from their debt.

I am told that you should not open ex-tenants mail, but let's just say if you did, what do you think you would find? I am very much taking an educated guess here of course, and say that you will find letters from other creditors like loan companies, credit cards, hire purchases and fines that have all gone unpaid. They walk away from that too to a certain extent, when they finally leave your property. As I said, it's a lifestyle some lead, using your rent money to pay for their non-essentials and lifestyle.

Cash Rich Prospective Tenants

You might think that a prospective tenant coming to you as a landlord offering to pay three months up front is a good thing. You may possibly even dream of this happening with all tenants, to make your life easier. It is quite astonishing how many times people can offer you several months in cash for their rent, although it is very likely to be the opposite of what you think it is.

I have had this on many occasions, and usually they are also in an apparent rush to get into the property. They try to circumvent your tenant vetting procedures by offering you the cash as the security. In these situations, you might well be looking at all the rent money you will ever get for the tenancy, as they are probably not going to pay you ever again.

This trick seems to be quite widespread with problematic tenants, at least the kind that are of the variety that want accommodation as cheap as possible by not paying you their rent money, when it is next due. It is easy to be lulled into this false sense of security by the sight of the cash. It might similarly be an offer to transfer money to your account as a payment of several month's rent in advance.

Where do you think that cash could have come from in the first place? Most likely I would say it is part of the money they did not pay to their last landlord and saved in their pockets or their bank accounts instead. That would be the money from the months after the time when the cash they paid them up-front ran out. It would be partly from the time they told their last landlord all the reasons they could not pay. Reasons which of course would likely have been stated as due to unforeseen circumstances, which would be addressed very soon.

'Very soon' never comes though, and these turn into the tenants who walk away from their debt, as just discussed. The cycle then repeats and catches out many landlords. At the same time, it saves the 'mobile tenant' many months in rent and they can feed their lifestyle with that money.

CHAPTER 2

Rights and Responsibilities

Regulations Get More Demanding

In the time I have been investing in property now, I have seen a vast increase in the amount of legislation introduced to make owning and letting out property much more onerous. And this is just in a space of less than two decades, with more legislation reported to be on the horizon. It seems relentless.

When I first started, at the turn of the new century, buy-to-let was the talk of the town. All we had to do from a contractual point of view was get a tenancy agreement signed. You then had the right to claim your property back if there were any issues with the tenant behaviour, or simply because you want it back. Nowadays we have to make sure there are many boxes ticked before doing that (even though you own the property), including demanding routes to registering and protecting any tenant deposit paid.

We could also charge for the administration involved in registering the new tenant to cover the costs of our time or the time or services of others (including taking references and credit checks). Recently, even this changed and despite the increase in the documentation required, the costs for covering tenancy set-up activity cannot be charged to the prospective tenant anymore.

If you researched the amount of legislation that applies to a landlord that is currently in force, you would be horrified. Nevertheless, ignorance is no excuse and you will have to educate yourself on this subject. Even if you give the task to an agent, the responsibility remains with you to ensure legal obligations are complied with.

Some of the duties carry the potential for a criminal prosecution, if not complied with. This is heightened if you go down the Houses of Multiple Occupation route, as I have done.

As most of you may be aware, the next thing that seems to be on the government's agenda is the removal of the right to simply ask for your property back after the end of a fixed-term contract. That is because tenant support groups claim that such a right has been abused by landlords in terms of 'revenge' on tenant repair requests. Whilst this probably has happened, I know most landlords would simply use it to remove problem tenants without having to prove the problem in court, which can sometimes be difficult to do.

After this new change will surely come another change, and then another, and then another. I can't image an end to this, it has become a worrying trend.

Tenant Protection Rights are Strong

It can easily take 3 to 6 months to evict non-payers. This is even assuming you get the paperwork right, which can be quite demanding as mentioned earlier. You can of course ask a solicitor to do all the legal work for you, but this will cost several thousand pounds in the end rather than paying several hundred or so if you do it yourself.

I have had a case thrown out of court for a simple error of £50 in my rent-owing calculation when the tenant owed several thousand pounds. However, the judge seemed to take great pleasure in protecting the surprised tenant who thought his time had finally come since the defence lawyer (one they can get access to on the day at court) could not otherwise defend him.

In fact, my lawyer knew they were going to concede the case and ask for 28 days to leave, rather than 14 days. How such a person can call themselves a Justice of the Peace by annulling a case because of such a simple error is beyond me, but that is the reality of it. The fact that the judge was visibly taking pleasure in pointing out the error, and letting the tenant get away with his wrong-doing, made it all the more a saddening thing to witness.

Even assuming the eviction paperwork is all done correctly, the difficulty in getting payment and evicting on the grounds of non-payment is well understood by most tenants. This means that they will take advantage of this situation and the payment of your rent money will not be their highest priority. There will be some tenants that play the system and make a lifestyle of paying very little rent all their lives.

You might think you can go and pester such people for the rent money. Well, you can, but then you have to be careful of any counterclaims for harassment. But by all means sail as close to the wind as you can on this one, because if you don't then the word will get around and maybe other tenants you have will start playing the same games. This can especially be the case in HMOs where tenants from one house may know tenants in another house owned by the same landlord.

Even as difficult as it sometimes is, evicting someone based on the tenant's arrears is the easiest eviction possible. The other most common thing that arises is antisocial behaviour. Theoretically, you can evict on these grounds but don't expect the judge to side with you based on the stories you present. Instead, you need hard evidence and ideally have some signed witness statements. Although you may get a lot of complaints from others, getting them to sign a statement is a different thing entirely.

You might think that the council or police will help with the needed evidence, but I have not found that to be the case. You will often hear the phrase 'data protection' somewhere being muted as a reason that they will not co-operate on this. Yet in the next sentence, they will tell you that you have to do something about the tenant's behaviour as their landlord. What a ridiculous situation.

Tenants Get More Rights

With every new piece of landlord legislation that comes in, there seems to be some increase in tenants' rights. Not accounting for how good the tenants are, simply because they are tenants, they get more rights. It would be better if this was based on the quality of tenants, but alas it applies to rogue tenants as well as good ones.

Shelter and the Citizens' Advice Bureau appear to be the main pressure groups pestering the government for the changes that result in more tenants' rights and more legal matters for landlords to deal with. In my experience, a tenant that pays well will also speak good about you as a landlord, but the many that don't pay well will call you all the names under the sun. The logic I put to this is that it makes them feel better for their tenant wrong-doings. Whereas, those not doing any wrong can only see good in you.

A poor-paying tenant is therefore likely to give a bad account of their landlord to the representatives of the pressure groups. The reality is that the landlord may have been nothing of the sort as described. The matter was an attack on the landlord without them being able to defend themselves. With the root cause being that the tenant was behind on rent and maybe wanted to move from their present premises simply because of that and start again.

The people in the pressure group organisations believe the tenant's lies (or at the very least, their exaggerations). It gets formalised through written reports and stories and makes most landlords look bad. Landlords are then judged without a hearing. I don't claim that all landlords are good but the vast majority I know only want to do the best they can for their tenants. There is only a small minority who want to exploit them, people I don't know personally locally, but know a few names which keep cropping up. You will get good and bad in all businesses, not just property; however, it seems landlords all get tarred with the same brush as far as these pressure groups go.

There is no end to this tenant-strengthening legislative onslaught in sight, I only see things getting worse until they break the private rental housing system when it is no longer viable to be a landlord. In fact, I hear increasing sentiment getting around landlords about how tough it is now, and this never used to be the case. Something will give in the end, but not sure when that will be. Only then will the government listen to common sense I expect, when it is too late (which seems to be an all-too-common trigger point).

Ineffective Landlord Representation

There are Landlord Associations that are large in terms of percentage representation of landlords, but these always seem to be defending (and often losing) assaults on landlords by the government and pressure groups. It is like being part of a union that has no real teeth. This is not a swipe at those genuine people who run these associations, it is just that they are not listened to or seemingly not respected enough to influence decision made by the government.

The poor public image of the landlord, as explained elsewhere, seems to dominate and weakens such professional representation efforts. Recently, the two largest national landlord associations have merged. These are the National Landlords Association (NLA) and the Residential Landlords Association (RLA), together forming the National Residential Landlords Association (NRLA), I hope you are still with me after that!

I would hope to see just the one larger association have a bigger impact and have one voice to support landlords. Time will tell on this one but I think the reasons I have stated already will mean that this is an uphill task, but someone has to carry it out. Only don't expect that you have the support you might think landlords should get, despite the people in these organisations being very knowledgeable and professional.

I remember on one landlord advice call, to the then-RLA, I was told that I just had to face up to the fact that a landlord is the underdog and that tenants tend to always have the upper hand in law. I will never forget that. However, I am not aware of any mission that is in place to restore the balance and the onslaught continues against landlords in favour of better conditions for the tenant side of the property letting relationship.

We need such organisations, however, and I would recommend you join up to support them, if only to get their often very excellent legal advice, even if it is not what you want to hear.

Small landlord organisations also operate in most areas on a local level and can be a great resource of defence against, or relationship-building with, the local council. I would say that these local organisations can have some impact on the local council decisions and I have experienced that first hand. Albeit this influence tends to be the exception and councils prefer to forge ahead regardless in general.

An example of a major success by our local landlord association was to block the introduction of Selective Licensing. This would have given the council more powers in the designated deprived localities, than would be available in national law. The idea was that these areas were deprived and needed such additional local rules. However, it was clear that this would not deliver anything much more than more hassle for local landlords as well as more costs, for very little benefit to tenants. We won, and I was privileged to be on the Committee for that two-year battle.

No Support from Environmental Health

When I first started managing my properties, I was faced with some challenging situations to manage as I learned the ropes. There were times when I felt out of my depth with unexpected problems that I did not have access to the right resources to deal with. The worst was when it was a health and welfare issue that needed sorting out quickly.

Naïvely, I expected the local council would be there for me to offer some help in such circumstances. This was to prove to be a false sense of security. I found this out with sudden rebounding force when I went to them for urgent help one time, this proved to lay down the nature of my relationship with them going forwards.

When I say 'them' I specifically mean the department at the council responsible for Environmental Health. You would expect that as the council, they would have access to the resources to deal with any threat to the welfare of people in their borough. At least that is what I reckoned when I called upon them for help with a blocked toilet pipe of a house I had let to a young single-parent with a family of three children.

It turns out that the toilet had been flushing more and more slowly for many days. Then the tenant reported it to me at the point that it would flush no more and the water was overflowing upon flushing the toilet. This of course puts a time pressure on it that would not have been there if I had been informed when it first started showing the problem.

I sent out the plumber as the first point of call but they could not sort it out. I then called others and nobody could offer a solution as the waste pipe was blocked solid up to the top of the first floor. At this point it seemed like nobody I was in touch with could help. I then made the mistake of contacting the Council's Environmental Health Department, who I had assumed would have access to plenty of resources to help.

I was somewhat shocked when they simply sent out a representative to the property to investigate and duly served a formal notice on me to sort it out within 48 hours, or face prosecution. Thanks for your help, Environmental Health!

To put this into context, it was early days in my property investing career and I was still working full-time and trying to sort this out during short work breaks. In the end, it was somewhat with a bit of luck that I found someone who would take on the task, by looking for them in the local directory of drainage contractors. I explained the situation to them and they gave it a high priority to attend to.

The lesson I took away from this is that there is no backup available from the local council if you are in the 'sh1t' and need support, they are only likely to add to your problems and try to prosecute you for it.

This was not the only such incident of this kind of problem which is often started by tenants putting 'wet wipes' down the toilet and then the wipes stick and accumulate in parts of the old drainage path. Needless to say, I never called on the council for help again and went on to manage it myself, no matter what 'sh1t' I might find myself in.

Criminal Liability

As a landlord, you will become both personally and potentially criminally liable for your action or inaction associated with running your properties. For the second listed liability, you cannot hide behind a limited company either. If you get something wrong this could be a showstopper for your life. Fortunately, we don't hear about this much at all, but you have to realise the risk is there.

Insurance will cover you for your personal liabilities, assuming you have both correct and adequate cover. You will not be able to cover yourself from any criminal prosecution, however. Once you have got a criminal record then you would have trouble in being a landlord of any HMOs as this would prevent you from that status as a property manager for them. You would have to find someone else to manage these for you.

HMOs carry a lot of possible criminal liability potential with them. Simply housing more than the stated number of people on the licence would be such a crime.

I could not even start to list the amount of laws you need to comply with here, that would be a separate book in itself but you may wish to research the subject yourself. This alone could be a pressure too much for some people, whereas others are not significantly affected by this as a pressure on what they do (or do not do).

One such requirement that would apply to all landlords is to have a gas safety certificate for your property. Should the worst happen and you did not have this in place then it would be you that would face criminal prosecution for the death of the tenant. You might think that this is fair enough until you try to get access to the houses of some tenants to do the certification for the gas boiler and other gas appliances check.

You will therefore have to keep one eye on how you can legally cover yourself when you cannot get the things done that you are legally obliged to do. Alternatively, you will need to get more focus on making sure these things do get done, which would be a safer position to be in.

Ignorance is No Defence

As indicated already, you are responsible for all the laws you should comply with as a landlord, and there are many. There will be no account taken of the fact that you did not know about one of them at the time a case of liability is brought against you. Ignorance is no defence, as you may well have heard the saying go before. It is as true for landlords as anything else.

This would even be the case if you are asking a letting agent to rent out your property for you. For sure you have another layer of management between you and the tenant but the ultimate responsibility still rests with you as the landlord of the property. In some cases, this can make it a little worse in that you are not involved in the detail of the day-to-day running of your property, but you remain ultimately responsible for it.

Your alternative is therefore to get to know the laws and comply with them to the best of your ability. You should take some specialist courses that are offered by national landlord associations on this topic and also join your local landlord association. In this way, you will be made aware of what is required of you as a responsible landlord. Be careful you do not simply follow everything you are told however; you should follow up and verify what you are told if you want to act upon it.

I have heard some incorrect statements from people who are very experienced in property management. Remember, you are still responsible for the validity of any information that you decide to follow, even if you have heard it from someone more experienced than you in property lettings. There is a chance they can be wrong, and why should you expect any different as they are only human and make mistakes or simply don't know everything.

It still amazes me concerning the number of laws there are and the requirements that need to be complied with, especially compared to the number of cases and prosecutions that are brought against landlords. This latter point is of course a good thing as if there is no case brought against you then you will not have to account for your acts or omissions, whether or not you complied with the law. Not that I am advocating ignoring your legal responsibilities, I am just saying that this is the case. This is a relief for us as landlords as we are not perfect despite our best efforts (even though this is still not a valid excuse).

Impractical Landlord Advice

Landlord advice lines are generally not practical in what advice you are given. This is not the fault of the people trained in housing and landlord law on the advice line, but rather the law is the issue. Remember, you are the one that has the disadvantage in nearly all situations in the tenant and landlord relationship.

The advice lines can only tell you what the law is in black and white and what you should do, by following the relevant laws. They cannot take any leeway and weigh-up matters as you will probably do, once you know what options are open to you. I am not supporting taking the law into your own hands here, but I am saying you are likely to have to take a common-sense decision after weighing up the pros and cons of taking this or that action.

When I had the local council managing my properties, they were even taking decisions that are not exactly in line with the law. However, these were seen to be necessary to keep things flowing and having the properties back in use rather than leaving these properties empty for long periods. Such action could not be advised by the advice lines as there would be a potential liability that would rest with them for giving that advice.

It only takes a few bad outcomes to cause an advice-line a huge problem, if legal action is taken against them for the outcome of advice that went wrong. The advice lines can't afford the damage this would cause in terms of loss of reputation about the advice they give.

I am very sure the advice the advisors on the landlord advice lines give every day is not the action they would be taking if they were in the same situation managing their own properties. This is particularly so concerning abandoned properties. This is quite a common problem and one that they will be giving a lot of advice out regarding taking the case to court. This is even though probably no tenant is there at the property to take such action against.

Having said all of that, I do use the advice lines because it is always good to hear what the legal situation is on any matter and understand the consequences of not doing it properly. I will then weigh matters up and decide for myself what I should do. Of course, my hard limit is to not do anything that could be considered as a criminal act, but many other matters are outside of this and would not be considered criminal.

For these matters, it is my prerogative to take my own decision by weighing up the possible outcomes and consequences, then taking the action accordingly. When I decide on taking a certain action, I have to be accepting of any financial or other penalties that could be imposed on me for doing so. This then becomes a business decision. There is no way that advice lines can help you make this kind of decision, even though that is really where you need to seek help from in your particular circumstances.

This is when the membership fees for your access to the advice lines from the National Residential Landlord Association pays dividends. It empowers you to take business decisions based on facts, rather than ploughing ahead and doing things with your head firmly buried in the sand.

Your Property Maintenance Obligation

You have to maintain a property even if the tenant is not paying rent or causing trouble; this is your legal obligation. It might not seem fair that you have to keep to your side of the contract if the tenant has broken and continues to break theirs. Who says laws are meant to be fair?

This is the reality, however, and although it is very uncomfortable when a bad tenant, you would rather not have, complains they have no heating in the middle of winter, you have to sort it out, and quickly. They might even be on the road to eviction or have a court order against them to leave. No matter what, you have to deal with the situation, or stand on the wrong side of the law.

There are things you don't need to do for tenants, such as change the light bulbs and change batteries in smoke alarms during a tenancy, unless it is the common area in an HMO. However, pretty much anything beyond this is your responsibility to ensure the maintenance of, and in a prompt manner.

Boilers are discussed as a separate matter as they tend to cause the main problem with property maintenance and keeping tenants happy. However, suffice to say that if you cannot fix a boiler straight away then you are obligated to provide back-up heating. You would think that such replacement heating is only required when the weather is cold and not in the summer. This may well not be the view of your tenants and whoever they night complain to. It is better to do too much rather than not enough to avoid any causes for criticism if you can.

You should also provide running hot water which is a more difficult matter to address in the shorter term. For that reason, it is advisable to have electric showers in your property to avoid this double-hit situation, when a boiler fails. This at least reduces the urgency of this matter somewhat. If all hot water depends on the boiler, you will be under increased pressure to address the matter in double-quick time.

I have not been happy to provide standalone water heaters due to the risk of these being knocked over. Of course, a house will most likely have a kettle or some means to heat water outside the provision of hot water from a boiler, but the tenants will not easily be able to provide hot water for bathing or showering during a boiler failure (unless you have an electrical heater shower installed, as just advised).

A study of your maintenance obligations in detail would be a separate study and even the subject of another book. Suffice to say, in letting a property out, you are taking on a considerable responsibility to maintain the property for the tenant. You can easily see how this can grow into a considerable burden as a landlord builds up a property portfolio.

It also doesn't matter what your personal situation is at the time of an urgent maintenance request. I had to deal with urgent boiler breakdowns when my mother was in hospital with a stroke, a hospitalisation she would not return from. I made the tenant aware of the situation in case it affected my response, which it did not as I managed to get it fixed within a few days as I recall.

However, later that year, the sister of the same tenant put in a claim against me for an alleged loose handrail, a story I cover in more detail later in the book. Just don't expect any thanks from some tenants for whatever you do for them under whatever challenging circumstances you may have to perform under.

CHAPTER 3

Taxation Attack

Taxation Gets Worse

When George Osborne was Chancellor, he brought in his "anti-landlord tax" (often more formally referred to as the Section 24 landlord tax), this was done at the same time as the 3% surcharge on stamp duty for second homeowners. The only difference was that the anti-landlord tax was phased in over 4 years; this was an attempt to slow cook you so you don't notice it until it is too late, I think.

This gradual introduction tactic shows the government knew it would have a significantly adverse effect on landlord financials. In Northern Ireland, this same punitive tax was brought into full effect overnight in times past but then was repealed as the effect was so devastating on landlords who were exiting the market. The UK government therefore learnt from that and craftily brought it in over four annual stages.

This introduces a massive change to the tax allowance on finance expenses used to purchase properties. It effectively now disallows interest on landlord finance costs (mostly mortgage interest for landlords) and replaces it with a 20% tax credit. This step therefore specifically targets the higher and additional rate taxpayers.

If you are a basic rate taxpayer, don't simply think it will not affect you, as the amount of your annual interest payment on your borrowing is now effectively classed as income (you read that right) and this is added to your other true income to get your revised 'theoretical' income. This theoretical total income is what is used to determine whether you are a higher rate taxpayer or not.

This tax is solely targeted at landlords owning properties in their personal name and using mortgages, as well as other sources of finance to acquire their properties. It in no way affects those individuals who are very wealthy in terms of simply investing their cash to outright purchase their properties. This is very strange since one of the statements from the government was that this tax will only affect the wealthiest of landlords. But the reality is quite the opposite.

In answer to this tax, most landlords are now looking to form limited companies, amongst other business structures. This however can cost a lot of money for existing landlords as in some cases they have to effectively 'sell' their properties into a company and pay the associated taxes. Other ways around this are being sold by tax advice businesses, although there are risks there about possibly falling foul of the General Anti Abuse Regulations; meaning if this is done solely to save tax, it can be disallowed.

New landlords are often advised to simply form a limited company in which to hold the properties to avoid this additional taxation. However, who is to say the government could not soon bring in the same regulations for property investment businesses. This tax was applied retrospectively to landlords owning in their own name, so the government could later do the same to property limited companies.

Even after operating your property business inside a limited company, you will face double taxation in terms of paying corporation tax before taking money out of the business as wages or profits in dividends. Let alone forgetting the fact there is no personal capital gains tax allowance available upon disposal of any property, when owning property inside a limited company.

Again, landlords are an easy target for unfair treatment because there will be no sympathy from the general public for any harsh treatment of landlords. The media see to it that the poor image of landlords is maintained, as it makes for good reading and increased sales of their news stories.

Wear and Tear Tax Allowance Removal

There has been a significant recent reduction in the tax incentives available to landlords. One of the big ones for some landlords was the removal of the fairly generous 10% wear and tear allowance. This allowed 10% to be deducted from the income as an effective business expense of replacing items subject to wear and tear in properties let out furnished.

This meant of course any actual costs for replacement goods and fittings subject to wear and tear could not be claimed for as well. However, overall it enabled a landlord of a furnished property let to take a careful approach to replacement management. By doing so they could then benefit from a very reasonable tax allowance that could, on average, be more than the expenses incurred. For those with large furnished portfolios, especially having high-income HMOs, the removal of this allowance was a major blow.

The change to this tax benefit is that you now have to simply apply the actual cost of the replacement items. Nevertheless, it does amount to a lot of money that is no longer available for the property investor to take out of the business. The difference between the 10% of income and what is actually spent is now subject to taxation.

This change didn't affect all landlords, as many do not furnish their properties. Where it is their option, fewer landlords will be letting out properties furnished with this tax incentive removed.

Additional SDLT Charge

Most will be aware of the additional tax charge on second home purchases as it was widely publicised because of the potential impact on the non-landlord purchaser. This is an additional 3% stamp duty land tax charge (SDLT) that applied to the full amount of the purchase. Normally SDLT is applied in bands, not a blanket amount, meaning this probably hits the typical property investor band of purchase prices the most.

Some specific situational exceptions exempt the application of the tax, such as on the purchase of very low-value properties below £40,000, but in all likelihood, the tax affects the vast majority of landlords. This might not be such a hard hit because at least it is a one-off cost and not something repeating annually. Nevertheless, it is another tax cost that we did not have before and can significantly add to the operational costs of a serial investor.

You may simply think you can just deduct this from your offer price to account for this additional cost and have done with it. I certainly take that view because all that matters is the total bill at completion in terms of what you paid to acquire the property. That total figure is then the investment that you need to get a return on, or refinance back out (if you are adding value and refinancing your deposit money back out later). Therefore, I would fully support that approach of deducting the additional tax charge from your offer.

However, the effect of this is that you are less competitive in your offer against most homeowner buyers, and might lose a few deals that you would have otherwise would have won. You will then have to work a bit harder to get some deals accepted at the prices that work for you and your investment strategy. In this sense, it ultimately becomes more of an additional resource pressure rather than a price pressure.

Either way, it is something we did not have to deal with before and it has made property investing that little more complicated and costly in recent times. Not a major impact overall, but significant enough to affect you. Even with the stamp duty holiday introduced to help get the property market through the coronavirus pandemic, the government left this additional surcharge in place. There seems to be no mercy for landlords, no matter what.

Property Investment is NOT a 'Business'

I have, once or twice, heard people phrase this in the form of a joke question, as in 'when is a business not a business?', with the answer being 'when it is a property business!' This is of course in the context of the taxation as the government treat landlords as being in an investment business rather than a conventional trading business.

This allows for separate property tax treatments to be applied which, not surprisingly, are more punitive than for typical trading businesses. It even extends to not getting the full benefit of reduced capital gains tax on the sale of your assets, unlike owners of trading businesses that get the full tax allowance. It also means you can't exit your business and benefit from the entrepreneur's relief the government introduced.

Most who actively work in property as their business will find this classification very insulting to the work they do. A lot of the portfolios run across the country are run either directly by the landlord or, in the case of the larger landlords, a management company may well be set up by them to help manage their properties for them. Of course, there are other landlords, mostly the smaller landlords, who will simply contract out the management of their properties, especially when these are away from the area in which they live.

The more sensible way to approach this would of course have been to set a definition on what would constitute passive property investment versus a property business renting out properties. The only definition of this is a precedent determined by a legal case, and there is no formal legal definition. It is preferred by the government to keep the definition of all property rentals as to be an investment rather than a trading business.

Given the recent attack on landlords with punitive taxation for those owning property in their own name, you will see a focus now more towards formally establishing such property businesses and using the legal precedent on this to defend that status.

In considering the government's general view on this however, it amounts to having a second-tier business when you are in the property business, but with more compliance regulation than most other businesses face to legally operate. Something does not seem right or fair here and I can't see any argument to support what is in place. That is apart from the misunderstood notion that large scale property investment is a passive investment requiring little business input from the landlord.

I know a lot of property mentors and teachers would also have you believe property investment is a passive income provider, but to me, that is a matter of marketing and does not reflect reality. Clearly, they can't tell you what I am telling you here and then expect to sell you their courses and mentorships to learn how to get involved. This is not to say you should not want to get involved in property, but these particular aspects are not conducive to you deciding to do so.

The passive property investment perception is thereby perpetuated, and much to our detriment as a landlord.

Punitive Capital Gains Taxation

As we have already touched upon, Capital Gains Taxation on selling a property is punitive compared to that applied to other businesses. For most people, the capital gain of property is a major motivator for investing in property in the first place. Don't get the idea that you can keep it all and in fact, you can expect to offer up more in taxation of your profit than any other business would have to do.

At the time of writing, a landlord would be charged 10% more tax for capital gain achieved than any other business owner upon the profitable sale of an asset. This will be affected by your marginal rate of tax as well, in the same way it would for other businesses. That is higher and additional rate taxpayers pay more tax than basic rate taxpayers, 10% more, currently.

At least there is a capital gains exemption amount per year that you can benefit from, albeit only if you own property in your own name. This however is the property ownership model that is being targeted by other taxation assaults right now with the notorious Section 24 anti-landlord tax, as just discussed.

I understand that things are going to get more challenging in this area soon, with talks of payment of capital gains tax being required to be made much sooner than it has historically had to be paid. This could therefore be an area for further attention by the government to take away more hard-earned money from landlords. Of course, the government doesn't see it that way, as it is just investment returns from passive investment as far as they are concerned.

More recently I have heard that capital gains tax for landlords will likely be increased further. As you can imagine, this would not surprise me.

No Offsetting of Losses Against Other Income

Any normal trading business can offset any loss they incur against the income they might have earned elsewhere, such as in their employment in another unrelated role. This situation would apply to many landlords that are just starting in business. In a property rental business, all you can do is offset any losses from the current year to profits in future years.

This will be of little value to you if you need to cover those losses and use other sources of after-tax money to support your losses. You might think it is not possible to make losses in property, but I can assure you that is very easy to do if you make a mistake or two in any given year. I have made losses in the past and I don't mind saying so. This was partly because I was so enthused when I first started, I went that fast I did not realise my business was not paying for itself like my predictions said it would on paper.

This situation of not being able to offset losses against other income is not the case in some other countries. In other countries, you can offset any rental losses against earned income and get a tax repayment from the tax you have paid on your employment income. One such country is Germany where I have known investors do this and sometimes, they invest to a level where they made losses in order to reclaim some paid income tax.

In this case, they are investing in the future when they won't have the earned income and it makes sense for them to do that. For example, repairing the houses to a high standard to reduce any major maintenance requirements for many years to come. I personally know of a particular German citizen doing this, who managed to retire early due to the strategy of investing to a level that lost money while he was in employment. He also used the tax he claimed back from the 'losses' to further build up a strong asset base that would pay him back later.

This can be very useful, but unfortunately, it is not available to property investors in the UK. Unlike if you had any other trading business where you could do this without any issue, at least for a few years until the HMRC may look into why your business is not making money. The idea of a business is of course to make money rather than lose it, but the ability to claim any losses back would be very welcome to most investors, especially when starting out.

Doing Your Tax Accounting

Taxes are currently annual affairs for the landlord although I have recently heard this could be changing to a quarterly affair. At the moment, the annual tax return that has to be done for your accounts as a landlord can be filed nearly 10 months after the end of the tax year. This being the case, you can easily guess when most landlords file their tax returns.

Let's put it this way, accountants are very busy at the end of January each year, which is approximately 10 months after the end of the tax year. It is not just landlords that are like this, also many other small businesses who leave things until the very last moment before submitting their tax return. After the end of January, you will incur a £100 fine if you file after that.

The fine does not seem to be a lot of money, but it seems to be enough to get most people to actually go and do the tax return that ideally they would have liked to have submitted 10 months before. The lack of being on top of their accounts fully is clearly the reason for this. Some people will be even as bad as to have just a bag of receipts and a bank statement with a receipt book to show income. Believe me, I have seen exactly this at my accountant's office.

There will also be those who keep records up to date, but only partial records. The most important record for the landlord is the record of rental income. The costs tend to come after that and might never be fully entered into the accounts until the final tax return is being done.

For most people with a sizeable portfolio of properties, they will get their tax accountant to do their tax return for them. However, the figures still need to be given to the accountant to work with. These have to be accurate and clear as well as having all the paperwork to back the figures up. If you are ever the subject of a tax investigation, you will suffer badly if you do not have an organised system for filing supporting documentation. You may be demanded by HMRC to provide this information.

All this leads to a big pressure which mounts for most people who prefer to do other things with their time rather than their accounts. For some reason, this seems to be true for most people, landlords are no exception. I have felt the pressure of this each year as I know I need to do it, yet still seem to find other things to do until it is screaming at me.

I would like to say I am better than other landlords on this matter, but I am afraid to say that I am probably quite typical actually. That does however allow me to feel the pain with many others who are like me. I for sure do not stand alone as you can see, and as my accountant reassures me (he keeps pushing for me to get the accounts done before his mad rush at the end of January).

Maybe you can be different and be more organised. Or maybe you just simply love doing accounts. By all means consider delegating this task, but then be aware of the large amount of money at stake if there is a mistake made that misses a major business cost for example.

CHAPTER 4

Repeating Problems

Renting Brings Out the Worst in People

In my experience, I have seen the combination of the notion that 'an Englishman's home is his castle' and the desire for the protection of a person's own wealth (however small) govern the behaviour of most tenants. These two factors of paying money and having a home to defend tend to bring out the worst in people I find, at least it does when they are your tenants. Tread very carefully when dealing with tenants, as these factors will be lurking below the surface in most cases, ready to explode at any unexpected moment.

When you hand over the keys to a property, you have no right to enter again at will, as many of you may already know. This differs for the common areas of HMOs, but let's focus on the majority of lets where this applies, namely single-let properties that make up the most of the letting units offered to the market. Immediately the keys to the property are handed over, you have a barrier to deal with about the behaviour of your tenant in your own property.

In addition, they have a contract with you that they should pay their rent at the agreed time, but there is no immediate threat you can put up in order to ensure they do this. Therefore, the payment of rent tends to come second to nearly every other money need that your tenant may have.

In the Coronavirus pandemic, this was further protected in law by creating a non-eviction period. I don't want to argue the rights and wrongs of this, but just to make the point that such action underlines the almost 'optional' nature of rent payment.

What makes my blood boil on non rent payment is the fact that I can lose a lot more money than can occur in a shop from shoplifting, or from someone driving away after filling up with petrol. However, these two wrongs are met with the full force of the law as a criminal act where the police can be called in immediately. Whereas the non-payment of rent is simply watered down as being a 'civil matter'.

Many programs on TV have shown that tenants can get away with major rent arrears and it is left to the landlord to instigate long and expensive legal processes for getting their property back. I think I have heard nearly every excuse under the sun for non-payment of rent, although I am sure there will be a few more new ones to surprise me. Normally, the tenant will add some kind of emotional connection to a reason for not paying their rent, but I think it is generally safest to take this all with a pinch of salt.

Common emotional reasons given to me by tenants for not paying their rent includes: not having any contract work to do or the tenant has just lost their job, needing to buy food, relatives needing money to support them, sick pets needing costly veterinary attention, or payment needed for major household items like large T.V.'s. My lost rent also pays for a lot of Christmas presents every year for people I don't even know.

As far as behaviour goes, they should look after your property according to contract. However, as stated elsewhere, the amount of deposit you are allowed to take in no way would go anywhere near to covering the amount of damage that can be done by a tenant. Before making any changes to a house, even simply repainting any part of it, they should seek permission. Although, the number of tenants that think they have a right to do whatever they want, simply because they live there, will probably not surprise you.

You do have some recourse to legal action upon unwanted changes to your property, but not many landlords take such action. In all likelihood, it would be hard to defend in front of a judge who would ask for all sorts of things from a landlord that would be hard to put on the table. The handing over of the keys is therefore the acceptance of the risk that you may well not get your property back as you gave it to them, in fact not even recognisable in the worst case.

To make it worse, the non-payment of rent and damage to a property often come hand in hand. In fact, I have some properties where I get less than the agreed rent but simply want to leave it with the tenant for as long as possible; I know it will be a full refurbishment project when I get it back. And at that I mean a literal gutting of the property and starting again. These cases are rare, but very significant when they happen, both in terms of cost and emotional impact on the landlord in feeling powerless except to accept the situation.

By way of some specific examples in the worst case or nightmare scenario, I can recall repossessing a property when the tenants left and had seven dogs inside the house. Outside was a series of kennels made of wood and breeze block, filled with a lot of dog waste (yes the 'sh1t' subject is back again, only a different kind of owner). Police had to be called to take care of the dogs and get the support needed to fully take possession of the house and change the locks.

Of course, the law tends to be on the side of tenants like this and makes it hard to recover your missing rent money, not to mention the cost of the damage done. These are the two things you should be aware of come hand in hand with having tenants. Do your referencing as well as you can, or suffer the consequences on an all too often basis.

Responsibility for Tenant Behaviour

Although a landlord legally has no direct responsibility for the behaviour of their tenants (there was recently a bill proposed that tried to bring this in, believe it or not), as far as other people and the local councils go, you just might as well have such a responsibility.

When a person who owns a house causes trouble or is antisocial in any way, they have a problem. If the person rents the house from a landlord, the landlord will bear the brunt of that problem. The neighbours will look to the landlord straight away to address the problem, and if that fails, they will immediately report you to the council who will then also look to the landlord to sort out the problem.

This is all despite the fact that the tenant will be of a responsible age and should take responsibility for their own actions. However, simply because you are their landlord it seems you have to be their care-worker as well. Notwithstanding the actions that can be taken against a person whether letting or owning a property, it seems the shortcut to take for some councils is to drag the landlord into the problem and insist they provide a solution.

Not only will neighbours and councils come against you, but any landlords affected also seem to join in the same game that they are often the victim of. Landlords of neighbouring properties may well be affected adversely by the behaviour of someone causing problems. They might find you on Facebook or by tracking you down on Companies House or using the Land Registry.

However, these groups will find you, and they will look to you to sort out the problem rather than have the council or police use the laws available to them to deal with antisocial behaviour.

Don't expect support from the police either. Even making noise outside of the hours of 7am to 11pm will not be seen as an issue for the police, although they are supposed to keep the peace in the community. Again, you may well to be pulled into these matters if the source of the disturbance comes from a property you own.

The local council have all the powers that they need and also have the support personnel to deal with such matters, but they still seem to prefer to pass the buck to the landlord with as much force as they can deliver. This is despite landlords not having the same level of powers (in fact very few powers) to effectively deal with tenant behaviour.

Examples of typical behavioural problems are tenants making excessive noise by either playing loud music or holding parties, excessive drinking and taking drugs, or creating a mess in the locality by storing rubbish or not emptying bins when they should.

Garden Sheds and Outhouses

Garden sheds and outhouses are an opportunity waiting to get filled with tenant waste. I know that most home owners would see these as useful spaces to store possessions that are suitable to store outside, but for rental properties these tend to be a magnet for tenant waste. In fact, it might not even be from your tenant if there is no lock on the door as waste from other sources will find its way in.

I have emptied enough of these spaces to know that they fill up again very shortly afterwards. Sometimes I have made many trailer journeys to the recycling centre for just one property, that is in the days when the councils allowed large trailers into these waste centres. It is very disheartening and a battle you will not win.

My solution has been to leave any such outhouses and sheds full of tenant possessions if it is not of a kind likely to harbour rats. This is when there are no soft furnishings or food sources present, otherwise it would have to be removed again to avoid attracting rats.

You can of course lock these up when emptied and even put screws in the doors. This will not deter the waste and rubbish from entering however. It will often result in damage to your property by forced entry which will then require repair work. This is a tough one to deal with, apart from to remove these storage places if you can. There are then no external areas to hide waste and unwanted possessions.

Should matters get really bad in terms of getting complaints from neighbours, the council is likely to instruct you to clear the waste away. You will then of course ask your tenant to do this. In my experience, it is sometimes difficult to get this done in a timely manner and the result is that the council will serve a formal notice on you as the landlord to get it done.

Here we are talking about dealing with bad tenants, but these do exist and more often than you may think. Good screening of potential tenants will of course help reduce the likelihood of this happening, but it is unrealistic to think you can be a sizeable landlord without ever encountering this on a repeating basis.

Weekend Breakdown Reports

Breakdowns or severe maintenance problems will often get reported late on Friday or on a weekend when it is hardest to find a tradesman to attend. This is not to say that this world is a strange place in that such things only happen at this time, but often tenants don't say anything until it is too late and approaching the weekend, when it becomes more pressing. This seems to be around the time when the tenants find time to bother reporting a problem, at the end of the week.

For example, a leak generally gets noticed but they don't report it earlier in the week, then as the week goes by, they decide to let you know on the Friday or even at the weekend when they are mostly at home. Only today in the early evening (a Friday) we got the report of a leak from a toilet coming through the kitchen ceiling. It is amazing how Friday and weekends become the urgent property repairs days.

Another example could be an electrical circuit tripping out which gets more frequent and can stop resetting after a while. Or a boiler tripping out that they repeatedly reset. On a Friday or at a weekend these become intolerable for tenants who insist they should be addressed immediately. This is of course exactly when most tradesmen are putting their feet up for the weekend.

If these things were reported as soon as something was noted that was not right, these problems could have been fixed during the week when the tradesmen are more easily available. The pressure to get some attention on these matters at the weekend is totally unnecessary, but seems to be a repeating theme you have to put up with as a landlord.

You might be able to get someone to call out at the weekend, although this is likely to be at an additional cost at an emergency call out rate. This then also becomes an extra but unnecessary cost to running your business.

Dealing with Damp

Damp is a general term used for all sorts of forms of moisture on floors, walls and ceilings of houses that sometimes leads to mould growth. In the eyes of tenants this will always be the landlord's problem and nothing to do with them as tenants. This is not the most exciting of topics as a property investor you might think, but it is one that might affect your income if you don't know how best to manage it.

There can be water getting in from the outside, and this takes two forms that you will have to deal with. The first is the most well-known one which is called rising damp. This is in houses that do not have a dampproof course and is common in houses from construction around 1900 or before, where there is no effective dampproof course installed.

In this case, moisture rises up from the foundation through the bricks and mortar and then comes through the plaster internal to the property. There are solutions to this which means you need to get damp-proofing installed at a significant cost. Having this already in place is normally a condition of obtaining a mortgage although after many years the damp proofing can break down.

You can easily identify rising damp by the fact that it is typically below 2m in height of the wall, as measured above the outside ground level. It often does not rise any higher than this and more typically in my experience it will not rise much more than 1 to 1.5m, so 2m is a very safe height to dampproof up to, if you are using a tanking system.

If you don't deal with this you can get claims of damaging people's health as it is surprising how many tenants have breathing difficulties affected by damp. Or so they claim, and their doctors will likely support it too. The good news is to deal with this you are just looking at a matter not much more than a few thousand pounds for an average rental house, not to count the redecoration costs later.

It would not be so bad if that is as far as it goes, however condensation is often claimed to be damp coming from the house. However, this is usually a matter of tenants drying clothing inside and not opening windows to ventilate. The hot, moisture-filled air, then rises and condenses out in the higher parts of walls, often in the corners of walls. Mould then grows on it and you get the complaints.

In my day as a young boy at home, my mother opened the windows daily and cleaned moisture from the window to control this. When mould grew anywhere on the walls, she would simply clean it off. Not much of this is done nowadays in general as the houses a lot of people live in are modern and well insulated and so condensation problems do not occur often.

However, in older houses that are more typical of rental stock, the lack of insulation to the walls tends to allow moisture to condense out and create the damp and mould problem. This is especially so if the windows are not regularly opened to allow the moist air to escape before condensing out on the walls.

When the tenants are paying for the heating this is not likely to be done, even though they should do it. They will be more interested in the bills for heating and happier to blame the problem on the landlord rather than their house management skills, if you can call it that. This often results in a standoff despite my efforts to educate the tenants on the matter at hand. I try to prove it by scratching away a little of the wall plaster to show it is dry underneath and just wet on the surface, but even that is not enough to convince them.

The mould that grows on top of the damp wall area only needs to be wiped off and sprayed with anti-mould spray costing just a pound or two from most hardware places. Try telling your tenants that though.

Bad Neighbours

You cannot choose who the neighbours of your rental properties will be. On the whole, you will likely have reasonable neighbours, depending on the areas in which you buy of course. It is good to make contact with your neighbours as they will be the eyes and ears to look out for you when you are not there, be sure to give them your phone number.

Giving them your phone number can backfire however if they are not going to be good neighbours to your rental property. You might get complaints from them, often together with a threat from them to go to the council about you if you don't do anything. As a good landlord you then just get on with addressing an issue only to get a call from the council as well. This will be because they called them straight away anyway. That is when you realise you have a bad neighbour who is probably out to cause you trouble.

Bad neighbour behaviour can also cause you other problems. Examples of this are having dogs creating noise problems or having a mess in their garden that truly attracts rats that then become a problem to your house, not to mention the unsightly mess for your tenants to look out upon.

Back on the subject of neighbours out to personally cause you trouble, you may want to look up some of my neighbours of an HMO I have in a reasonable area close to a nice park. It seems HMOs are not welcome on their patch. Some of what they say seems very discriminatory, but this is an example of what you can face. Simply google 'Say No To HMO' to meet my rental house neighbours. This campaign was started when I opened an HMO literally on their doorstep. I can't start to tell you how much hassle they have caused me. Yet nothing wrong has been done by me.

A bad neighbour can affect the rentability of your property, which can affect your income. This will be both in terms of void periods being extended as well as the amount of money you can get for renting out the property. The frustrating thing is that you are not in control of this, although you might try to take some action to address the bad neighbour. Good luck with that.

Bad neighbours have the habit of sticking around it seems, even when they are the tenants of a house and not home owner occupiers. The more you seem to wish them to leave, the more entrenched they seem to get. Maybe there is some logic to this if they know they are upsetting you and take pleasure from that. You would be surprised what makes some people tick. Nonetheless, anecdotal or not, it seems to be the case to me.

Of course, it comes as a great relief when a bad neighbour leaves. But what can be worse is that the next neighbour tenant is worse than what you had in the first place. Things that make a neighbour-tenant a bad one can be various things, but some examples would be noisy tenants, untidy tenants (outside mess and rubbish piling up), trouble-causing tenants who are outspokenly disruptive, and drug-taking or, quite often in my experience, excessively-drinking tenants.

Neighbours in my classification include those who live above or at the side of a flat you may own in a block of flats (or at the side of your flat). In this case, the main issue is of course noise disruption. If you have tenants in this situation, you will find they won't be staying long and you have the issue of more frequent voids which affects your income, not to mention the complaints from the tenant you have suffering from the noise. Such noisy neighbour-tenants does not always mean they are unreasonable people.

If they are unreasonable then the noise will be coming from playing music and having the television volume on loud. Or it could be deliberately being heavy footed as they walk around an apartment directly above yours. Even in the case of no such deliberately disturbing behaviour, a neighbour-tenant above your flat can just have a heavy flat-footed walk. I have heard these families of people being referred to as a herd of elephants, I think you get the picture.

Whatever the issue with a neighbour causing an issue, it is the helplessness you feel when you are faced with this that is very frustrating, as well as costly too.

Abuse of Cellars

Cellars in houses are somewhat like sheds and outhouses that tend to fill up with tenant possessions and/or waste. What can make these a little worse however is that water can get it and add damp or water damage to whatever is stored there. In the past, for houses dating around 1900, these could have been storage areas for the house and sometimes the place for coal as the fuel for the heating for the house, or even food storage and preparation in some cases.

Water can be worse if there is a high water-table in the area. This means that, depending on the season, the cellar will take in water as the water table rises. This can also be a cause of damage to tenants' stored items. It is therefore essential that you point out the cellar is not to be used for storage of possessions, or you will most likely be asked to replace any damaged items.

Storage of items in this area can also be a fire risk and you should have an interlinked smoke alarm fitted in the basement if it is possibly going to be used for any storage at all. This includes for storing the tenant's items, even though you might be advising your tenants they are not allowed to do this.

Admittance to the cellar area is likely to be required for access to the services such as gas supply and electricity supply. The electrical trips are also likely to be placed in this area if the incoming supply is in the cellar. This is quite normal for houses having cellars of a traditional construction from around 1900. Therefore, simply closing off access to the cellar is unlikely to be possible to do, unless the services control points and isolations are relocated to be accessible elsewhere.

No matter what you say to a tenant about the use of the cellar, if you have one in a rental house then you are likely to inherit unwanted possessions or waste from a tenant when they leave the house. If you don't want this to happen the you would be advised to at least make a point that you expect the cellar to be cleared. Also make sure that it is shown on the inventory that it was clear at the time the tenant moved in. Alternatively spend some money on shutting off the cellar for access and moving the service points to a different place so access is not required.

It has in fact been common practice for cellars to be infilled or blocked off over the years. If I am looking around a house then I am keen to find out if there is a cellar or not. If there is then I would prefer it to be one that can be converted into a usable room with daylight. Otherwise I can see that it could be more of a liability than an asset, and I need to take that into account when deciding which property to buy and what to offer.

Neighbour Wall or Fencing Issues

When you buy a property that has a wall or a fence as a boundary with a neighbour, there will be a description in the deeds or land registry document that will describe who is responsible for the boundary. These are normally marked out with 'T' markings to clearly show who has responsibility for its maintenance. However, you might not like the fact that a neighbour can put up what fencing or wall they like if you don't like what you see.

Another matter is that you might not like the way the wall or fence is being maintained and this can all lead to conflicts. Again, the old saying that an "Englishman's home is his castle" becomes abundantly clear in its truth, even when that person may not live in that castle, but just own it as a landlord. Resolving such matters therefore can become a point of stress and bad feeling if there is no easy solution as each person has a different point of view.

In the case of old terraced houses, the rear of these houses used to be open space but more often than not these have been fenced off for privacy and to give each property some personal outdoor space. There is still a requirement to allow access across these fenced off areas in this type of housing, although some might go a little further than they should and block such access, or make it difficult to cross.

When this is done, there can be issues regarding the waste bins that will need to be stored in a place where they can be put out for collection. In cases where the house is right on the path or curb, this can cause some issues that are hard to resolve. You not only have this issue as the landlord, but the tenant will have the issue to deal with and might refer back to you to have it resolved. No easy matter to deal with.

In some cases, you might have to take the lead and repair or replace a fence or wall that is not legally your responsibility. You may want to do it for the good of your property and the owner of the neighbouring property does not want to contribute in terms of payment for the work. That will have to be your decision to take, based on what you think it delivers for your property in return.

You can't force someone to do something even if they have a responsibility for such a thing, although you can try if you want, but with the services of a solicitor. However, you would end up paying more in solicitors time than it probably would cost to address the matter yourself in time and effort. It is not a matter of black and white in many cases, there is often a shade of grey involved and when this is coupled with a non-cooperative neighbour you have a difficult problem. Legal action may not be the best option, and other action very difficult.

Fencing and walls also used to be restricted in height to 2 metres, otherwise these would have needed planning permission to legally erect. However, when I was affected adversely by an overbearing fence that a neighbour tenant had erected, the council said there was nothing that they could do because it was now classed as permitted development. I will now have to decide if I have to take this up with the neighbour's landlord. This would be at the risk of a legal battle, as it affects the access to the rear of my property, in addition to the overbearing aspect it has to it. I am taking steps to avoid legal action the best I possibly can.

This is not what I really expected to have to deal with when I started investing in property. However, it has become a part of what needs to be addressed and it comes with the territory, so to speak.

Lack of Police Support

As touched upon before, you may expect the police would be there to support you when things go wrong, well you could well be wrong about that. You will be very wrong if you are looking to prevent something bad from happening. It seems they are only interested in investigating cases where something has actually happened and an actual crime can be investigated.

Most matters you might contact the police about will be thrown back at you as a landlord to deal with. As an example, I had a furnished let with everything in it needed for comfortable living. The tenant had stopped paying their rent so they had a few visits and letters to ask them to get back on track with rent payments. It seems they had a very different solution in mind.

On one visit that was being made, the door was open and someone was inside who was not the tenant. This person was asked where the tenant was and the information given was that they were in the process of moving out. Sure enough, just at that time the tenant came back and was confronted by a request, by my then-agent, to pay the rent and give formal notice that they were leaving.

The rent arrears were actually transferred by mobile device on the spot, which was quite a surprise. The keys were handed over and the tenant promptly left as the property inspection started. The reason they left quickly was clear. This was because they had taken most of the belongings that were part of the original tenancy agreement or replaced them with inferior goods, presumably swapping these out at the place where they were moving to.

Some of the goods were still there but damaged. The walls had been painted in places in multi colours that you would not have wished on your worst enemy. At this point I instructed that the police should be called because of the criminal damage and theft. The police came and spoke to me on the phone saying that I should have taken a deposit to cover the amount of damage caused (clearly, they were not educated in tenancy law and don't know about the cap on deposit levels).

I spoke back to them and insisted this was theft and criminal damage and they should deal with it that way. Because this was true, they withdrew their verbal deposit challenge from me and started to treat it as a serious matter. In the end there was a prosecution proposed but that turned into something they call restorative justice, with a payment towards the costs made, although not enough to fully cover the damage.

This is just one example; it would be another book to write about my experiences with the police and the lack of support available. However, I hope this serves to illustrate two points. These points are that police are not always right when they speak to you (just assume they are trying to avoid helping you), also that you should assert your rights as you believe them to be. If you are wrong, you can always back down later when you find out that this is the case.

Unfortunately, there are many cases that they simply call 'civil matters' and the police won't get involved to help you at all.

CHAPTER 5

Lifestyle Impact

Your 24/7 Police Service

You may well read the above as the police providing the 24/7 service to you. This is of course how it is intended to be in order to police society. However, what I am really pointing out here is that the police also expect *you* as a landlord to be available 24/7. They will seek you to help them 24/7 in any tenant matters such as a missing person investigation (usually they are just staying with friends). OK, maybe they don't try to contact you inside normal sleeping hours, but all other times are fair game.

That is of course until it is a change of shift and it's time for them to clock off. The urgency then seems to change suddenly in my experience. As a responsible landlord, I actually do want to support the police in their duties but it has worn a bit thin on me nowadays I must say. Added to this that, as landlords, we don't to get the support from the police that we would like.

It is always with a bit of a hesitation that I take a phone call if I get a 'no number' calling me and it is in an evening or at a weekend. During the week and office hours this is more likely to be a conveyancing solicitor or the local council trying to contact me over some matter that needs my attention. At a weekend the best guess is it could be the police wanting some information from you about a tenant, or about a tenant incident they think you can help them with.

There are times when of course it is serious and needs your attention, but for some other inquiries, I am sure the enquiry could wait until normal working hours and not out of hours or at a weekend. That is not how the police work however and they will tend to fit you into their working pattern, which is whenever the officer working on the case is at work. That can be at a weekend, bank holiday, or whenever.

Who's Calling You?

As you will have just realised, the police, council, and solicitors all hide themselves by using withheld numbers. This means you don't know whether to answer their calls depending on where you are when they call. Not only that, but assuming you take the decision not to take their call, you won't know which organisation to call back let alone which person you need to speak to.

For me, it is usually the solicitor that I would prefer to be speaking to as they are representing my interests. In a situation like this, when I don't know who is calling and I am currently dealing with a property matter with the solicitors, I return just one call to my solicitor to check if it was them calling me or not. The others can call me back if they still need to speak to me, as normally it is something that can wait.

This lack of display of the caller's number does however cause some inconvenience that you will have to manage as a landlord. There are other organisations or even individuals that might try to contact you using a withheld number to add to the complications it causes. Most recently I had a tax adviser's salesman using this tactic of concealing their number from me, because I had not previously answered his calls due to my lack of interest in the service he was trying to sell to me.

If you have only one or just a few properties, this is not likely to be a major problem. Although if you have a considerable number of HMOs you are more likely to have regular calls from the police or the council. Whatever the size and nature of your portfolio of properties you are likely to have these calls to deal with at some point.

For some people, this will be a distraction they can cope with and not let it affect them. Although for others it might be a matter of concern that upsets their day if they don't find out who is actually calling them when they can't find time to answer. Nor can they know who they should call back to find out who was calling and for what reason.

Others Are Better Than You

If you have any element of competitiveness inside of you, you could find comparing your progress with others quite frustrating. The social media abounds with the success stories of others in property and it comes at you thick and fast. You can't compete with a crowd of people like that who are all showing how successful they are with their latest projects. It could be quite a pressure for some who can wrongly think that others are all better than them.

It will be best for you to focus on one main investment strategy yet you will be hearing of others having successes in other strategies; this might challenge you in what you are doing and could send you off course. It can at the very least create a distraction and put doubts in your mind as you see the successes of others with different investment strategies working out.

You will of course only see the result of their work and to compare yourself with that might not be fair. You don't know what support they are getting, don't know what money they have behind them, what family help they have behind them or anything else very much about them. All you know is what they have posted. Even that could emphasise the good side as it is unlikely that many will reveal any shortcomings (although some are happy to do that too, which is quite refreshing, but not that common).

You might also put yourself under pressure to be something you would like to be, but to be so literally overnight. This could be far from where you currently are as an investor. The shame is, although many do wish to be serious investors in property, not that many actually find the resources to achieve it. I don't have any official figures but I think the numbers of people moving on from attending property courses to being successful in property in terms of actually investing, is in single figures.

There is therefore a big risk of never getting started, let alone never being satisfied with your progress compared to others. If you do get moving, the more you progress in property investment, the more likely you are to mix with others who have achieved greater things in their property lives. This means the bar is continually being raised.

You could see this as a good thing in that it ensures an ongoing challenge to help you grow. Or you could see this as a road to continuous pressure to perform beyond what you are comfortable with. How you respond to this depends on how you are as a person, and in particular how you compare yourself to others.

Property is a 24/7 Business

Following on from what was said before about property *not* being a passive investment, as many make out it is, I would go further and say it is a 24/7 business. If you love it then that will not be a problem for you, but if you have other priorities in life there might well be a conflict. As stated before, you can farm out some of the work, but you can never farm out the responsibility you have as an owner and landlord.

I know many people who leave property investment simply because of this fact, so I think it is very well worth a mention here as one of the downsides. We all have different personalities so what is OK for one person may be a huge problem for another. Some can shut off more easily than others when there is a space to take a short break from it. You have to know yourself and know how this might affect you.

Being a landlord direct to tenants is the most active way you can be involved. More will be expected of you if you have direct communication with your tenants. The best place to be to shield yourself a little is to have an agent or someone else between you and your tenants. At least that gives you some thinking time if you have a sudden demand or a problem. Otherwise, you will need to be very good at thinking on your feet as one wrong word can cost you dearly, your tenants will hold you to whatever you say, whether it was a slip of the tongue or not.

You could say something that could upset them or you could refuse something they think you really should help out with. Once you are seen as being a bad landlord by them it will be hard to shake off that image. If this happens then expect more interruptions on a 24/7 basis. With modern communications, it is hard to hide away from contact from an insistent tenant.

You might also want to keep up with what others are doing in property and take to social media and other forums for information and community, so you never really get a break from it, it becomes a 24/7 lifestyle.

Phone Calls at Inappropriate Times

You will get demanding calls at very inconvenient times. You might be focussed on doing something else when a call comes in and you might not be able to screen the call before taking it. It is amazing how inconvenient difficult tenant phone calls can be at times when there is a property problem, be prepared for this invasion into your life. Accept that is the price to be involved on the frontline in this business. Tenants are good at changing phone numbers so you might not realise it is an existing tenant, assuming that would have affected whether you answered the call at that time or not.

It is also a problem if you don't take the call just in case it is a genuine matter of urgency. You therefore tend to take the call even at inconvenient times. Having taken the call, your attention is then diverted to the problem at hand. This can be an interruption on your personal life as you are likely to feel duty-bound to deal with the matter at hand, rather than carry on with what you were doing, even if it was not an urgent matter as such.

Examples of times I have had to take calls is when I was on the way to the hospital when my late mother had just had a stroke, calls while at airports on the way to board for a plane, and while at social events or with friends trying to relax. Not to mention taking calls when you are in bed, in a different time zone, on a different continent maybe. It all happens.

As already said, you can minimise this by having an agent working for you. The fact that the agent takes the call can minimise the number of calls as well, but this will not stop these entirely as you might then have to be contacted by the agent about what the matter is about. It therefore reduces but does not eliminate such calls at inappropriate times.

There is a Lot to Learn

Aside from the legal side of things, there is a lot to learn in how to manage properties as well as managing the tenants we have inside our properties. I have already stated that housing and money tend to bring out the worst in people in my experience. You will have to deal with what you would not have to face in a life of not being a landlord. This is not to say that everyone is like this and in fact, some people are great tenants, but I normally take that to be the minority.

The key is not to trigger any conflict with your tenants and keep them happy so as not to stir anything that could take out vengeance on you. Believe me, vengeance often won't be far below the surface and you had better take care not to disturb it in them. After all, the tenant will have more power in a situation to control it than you will if you do trigger something that results in a kind of conflict between you and them.

Property investment is never text-book-like either, you can read all you want and go on all the courses you like, but the way things turn out can be quite challenging at times. Whether that comes from the nature of the property or the nature of the tenants you are housing. Either one can be a challenge and you are the one that will be left with the problem to solve.

As an example of something you probably won't find written about anywhere else, I recall taking on a flat which was on the ground floor of a converted terraced house. I refurbished the place and re-plastered and dealt with all the damp. I could not, however, avoid noticing the trail of slugs on the carpet. This seems to be something you will often see in long-term unoccupied properties, but once occupied these problems normally seem to go away.

Not with this property though, it seems these were nocturnal slugs as the first tenant I had in there would come back in the living room in the night and find slugs on the floor. Maybe six or seven of them at a time. Clearly, they were upset and distressed at this and my property was rightly blamed immediately. This was shortly followed by me personally being blamed for the problem after I could not resolve the matter straight away. I took actions and advice but nothing would cure this problem.

Taking further thought to the matter, I decided to get some expanding foam and squirt it down the gaps in the skirting board (even though such gaps appeared to be only at the top of the skirting board, and not very significant). Amazingly this seemed to cure the problem as it effectively sealed off wherever they came from. So, you see you might have to resort to your own ingenuity, as well as seeking advice at times, on matters that seem like they are out of control.

Management of Antisocial Behaviour

We have touched upon this subject before, but here we go in to a little more detail on it now.

It is hard to prove antisocial behaviour, despite how the complainants will make it sound a simple matter you should just get on with. Given the data protection laws nowadays, the council nor police will want to back up anything with evidence either. However, they will still look to you to sort the problem out. This is not in line with how the law on eviction for antisocial behaviour works however.

The reality of the alleged bad behaviour needs to be determined in a court of law by a judge, and the judge will need the information to base a judgment upon. The judge will come from the point of view of defending the tenant and they will have to be convinced otherwise, which may not be an easy task to achieve. I have been warned about this time after time when I have considered the legal route of going to court about antisocial behaviour reports.

In any case, you will need to bring the reports of antisocial behaviour to the attention of your tenants. You will need to point out that if the reports are true, that would be a breach of their tenancy agreement and could result in loss of their tenancy if proven correct. That would be a starting point of what would be a long-winded route to eviction however. If you are lucky, that will be enough to create the required change of tenant behaviour, although by experience I would not hold out much hope for that to be the cause to be honest.

When you do engage with your tenants, be prepared for a different story to what you have been hearing so far. There are always two sides to every story and to some extent you then have to engage some judgment over what you are hearing from both parties. Sometimes, you could just be getting brought into what is essentially a neighbour dispute and as the landlord you are being used to add pressure on your tenants. This is simply because it is seen by the neighbour as a way to cause more friction.

In other cases, you could find that your tenants are telling you a story that is simply a lie in defence of their antisocial behaviour. That is all well and good if the matter is addressed in that meeting, it does not matter who is telling the truth as long as the alleged behaviour is no longer a problem going forward. Or it could be the start of a long and complicated argument that you could get embroiled in. The council may be happy to stir it and simply repeat what they are being told by any complainants verbatim.

Although you are not legally responsible for your tenant's behaviour, you might as well consider that you are, that is in terms of the expectation on you to sort out such problems of antisocial behaviour of your tenants. As stated before, the government bill for the law that was supposed to make this a legal duty of a landlord was thankfully abandoned.

Bloody Boilers

I have to refer to boilers as 'bloody boilers' because my heart sinks each time I hear of a problem with any of these. The new boilers are not as reliable as the older boilers. These modern boilers are also more complicated and faults are therefore harder to diagnose. I often wish it was the case that the boiler was the responsibility of the tenant to maintain, but that is only ever going to be wishful thinking.

I know there are some exceptions where there are rentals of houses that exclude the maintenance of such equipment, but this is very rare. I won't deal with that here because it is not very common and by and large the boiler is the maintenance responsibility of the landlord.

So, these bloody boilers, can be the bane of a landlord. It is probably the most common cause for a maintenance call that you will get. It seems to happen the most when the boiler is needed most, in winter. In fact, the most vulnerable time you have with boilers is in extreme cold when you would expect they should be designed to hold up. Instead, with modern boilers, the condensate often freezes and blocks the condensate pipe. There is then an automatic shutdown of the boiler which will stay that way until the condensate is defrosted. This will usually need an engineer to call, depending on where the boiler condensate pipe is located.

For this particular issue alone, I recall having five calls in one snowy day on the coldest day of the winter a few years ago. In each case, it was the condensate that had frozen up. You would think that such matters are designed into boilers but that is not the case and you inherit that design problem as a matter of maintenance to deal with. Thankfully, I had an obliging heating engineer who had winter tyres on his wife's car that enabled him to go and do the necessary to save the day on each case.

Boilers come with a range of guarantee periods which are typically from one or two years up to five or even seven years. When the boiler fails in terms of an internal part failure, you can call on your guarantee. This would however require that you have the boiler registered at the time of installation with the manufacturer. This is not always done and so it is another task you should chase up with your installer after commissioning the boiler. Do this ideally before you settle their bill.

Even when the boiler has been installed correctly and the guarantee registered, the documents to prove this needs to be kept safe and given to the supplier's engineer to check on his arrival. In addition, there needs to be documented proof that the boiler has been serviced every year since the installation, or at the very least it has to show it was done within the last year.

The other thing is that manufacturer guarantee call-outs can take some time to get attention and it can be several days before the supplier's engineer can schedule a visit in. The positive is that the manufacturer will have all the required parts with them to carry out a repair, whereas a local engineer would likely have to order the part after diagnosing the possible problem.

In some cases, especially when a local engineer has to attend, such as if the boiler is not under guarantee, you will have ordered a part only to find that when it is fitted the part is not the root cause of the failure. This will result in additional time and expense and additional tenant frustration at the boiler not being repaired in a timely manner.

The most common boiler 'problem' however is the loss of heating water pressurisation. This just requires the boiler topping up in water pressure and maybe some air bleeding from radiators. Homeowners will sort this out themselves, but tenants will look to the landlord to fix the problem for them, so you get calls about this as well as true breakdowns.

I could go on but hopefully that gives a flavour of the specific hassle that modern boilers pose.

Property Addiction

Despite everything that I am saying here, all this does not put people off investing in property and for those who do take to it, they can often get to a level that seems like an addiction. On that topic, I recall having a forum debate with someone who said they were looking to stop property as they were approaching retirement. In the end, we concluded that in fact property investment was their life and not a job as such.

Despite their age, they found they enjoyed working in property investment so much that they did not want to stop and wanted to carry on into retirement. This is great if that is what you want from your life, although I would remind people that when they started out they had a reason to do property, and it would probably not just have been for the love of it.

You might think that this is not a problem, however I just worry that such people might get towards the end of their lives and finally remember why they got into the property business to start with. Having done that, it could be too late for them to enjoy what they wanted to do with their time, before property came into their life and effectively took over.

Certainly, you can see that there are many aspects to property you can get very involved in, for some people that is something they take to very well and enjoy. Or there might be some of the positives of property investment that even makes all the hassle that you can get very worthwhile for them.

Whatever the individual reason, property investors should be aware that it can easily take over their lives. There are also many property investor communities that makes your involvement in property somewhat of a competition and that could become another reason for keeping on going. There will always be someone you can look up to and wish you were in their position, which might become a reason to keep on going and going.

Be careful that if you get into this situation and want to keep on going in property, do this in a totally considered way and make sure you are happy that when you get to the end of your life you would not have wanted to do anything else instead. After all, many people get into property investment with the promises they hear of financial freedom and all that this can bring to a person, to enable them to do what they want to do. It is likely that working in property all their lives was not what they originally had in mind at the time.

Family & Friends

Maybe this is well known, but just to state the obvious in that case, you probably won't get any support for your property ventures from family and friends. You in fact might have to go find some new friends, possibly even find more family if the present one divorces you. Seriously, I have known great problems inside families when one person wants to get into property investment and another one does not.

I recall being in a property training course way back in 2005 and the teacher there was explaining how he had to get a divorce. This was because the tension between him and his then-wife was so great as he wanted to press ahead and she was somewhat risk-averse. Ironically, the result was that the divorce settlement meant he had to give over 70 properties to her when the divorce finally went through. Maybe this was not exactly what she had in mind!

Regardless, this was quite a shock to me considering myself happily married at the time and I was very scared about the idea of a marriage and family breakup. I found it hard to relate to the property teacher because of this and wondered how on earth he got through that phase of his life. Then within five years, I found myself going down the very same road that the property teacher had gone. So, believe me, this is a real potential family hurdle.

On the 'friends' side of things, it is really just a matter of understanding that you will not be able to share things with your friends about what you do. The investment in property is a totally different mindset to what most 'normal' people possess and they simply won't relate to you. If anything, you are likely to get negative comments when you could do with positive uplifting support. You will need to find new friends who are investors, or at least understand what you are doing.

It is also a real possibility that within five years you could be looking for a new family to supplement your new friends. No kidding. You will have to either check whether your family are really ready for what you want to do, or risk losing the family you have. Friends however can more easily be replaced and it would be better that you seek out different friends who can support you in what you do anyway.

I have to add that the family matter is not something you should expect, but that you should be aware is a real possibility. Your reaction to this will depend on how much you value your family. If you are anything like me it will be something you will not want to risk, then again, you may a dream you need to live out in property investment. If you take the risk, and if there is a relationship conflict, before you know it you are looking for another life partner.

Not to mention the effect this can have on your children, should you have any. With this will come guilt that you will have to manage, and that can be another emotional drain you will need to have the energy to cope with.

Property can therefore be a life-changing experience in more than one way, maybe not quite the way you were thinking of originally.

CHAPTER 6

Local Councils

Councils Will Use You

Antisocial behaviour is quite common in and around high-yielding properties that are typical for investors to buy. That is because these investment properties look excellent on paper and you can't seem to lose out on making good money. However, as we have seen before, the more money you make the more hassle you are likely to get.

The hassle will not only be your problem to deal with but also it will be a problem that is soon reported to the council. In fact, when you hear about an antisocial problem, you might not be the first to hear about it as the neighbours will normally call on both you and the council to address the problem at the same time, as you have heard me mention before. The council will look for a solution as soon as they can and they will not care what the cost or inconvenience is to you, they will just want something done.

They often seem to look for the quickest way to get the problem off their desk and won't be too bothered about the root causes of problems. That means one solution they will ask you for is for you to move the tenant away from the location of the problem. This will likely mean using another of your properties to move them to. They won't consider using any of their own housing resources as this would be taking on a problem tenant that they would then have to deal with themselves.

I have had this situation several times with the council pestering me to move the perceived problem tenants. The problems that were being reported could not even be substantiated and they were just going on neighbour reports, although I understand there was some police involvement at one time, which led to nothing. After they repeatedly refused to accept these tenants into council housing, and after the tenants said they also wanted to move, I relocated them.

What happened then is what you can typically expect, no further support from the council was given to the case, not even to get their rent payment back in place quickly after moving them. All things considered, including the refurbishment required after they left the old property, the void period during this time, and a cost for the degrading effect of the house that they were moved to will have cost me around ten thousand pounds I would estimate. Then of course the tenants cause problems at the new place and the council asked me to move them again. Not likely.

Even when I remind the council of the previous action, which they have got fully documented (less, of course, the amount of financial loss to me) they still insist that I should help in the same way again. So far, I have just held out and asked them to get support to help the tenants with their social problems rather than just move them on to create the same problem in a different location. This tends to fall on deaf ears at the council and they continue to pester to have a solution and request that I serve notice on the tenants.

If you do bend to the council and follow such initial requests, you will very likely do so at a significant cost to yourself and just address the problem for a short period, only for it to re-emerge again later.

Dealing with Council Departmental Conflicts

It can be confusing working with the local council because different council departments can have different opinions and ideas about the same things. This is particularly the case when it comes to housing standards officers, building control, and the planning department.

It is entirely possible that if you deal solely with one of these departments on a project about all relevant matters, you would find that another department would disagree and ask for something else. It is therefore necessary to involve all of the possible stakeholders from the council in any project at the outset. When you get conflicts in requirements, you will have to facilitate the resolution of these matters as it is unlikely that they will speak directly to each other about it.

This might come as a surprise, but it is the nature of the matter in that the council departments tend to operate in silos, but you have property projects that command involvement from several of these silos. The outcome of what you do in property development at any level will be of interest to the above-mentioned relevant departments.

Within each particular department, you may even find differences in interpretation and enforcement of relevant guidelines or requirements. This is also at a personal level where the personalities and experience of each person with key roles in each of these departments will influence what you are told. Also don't expect things to remain the same and be aware of how departments do or don't work together, can change.

One example of this that I can give you is where it was quite possible, several years ago now, for me to have an HMO licensed up from 6 people to 7 people without the involvement of the planning department. That was because I could show I had been operating the HMO for many years without complaint and they would then consider it as an established HMO. As long as the welfare requirements were met in terms of kitchen and sanitary arrangements, they would sign off the increase for me and this would then appear on my HMO licence for that property.

However, this is now a matter of sharper focus with the housing standards department, and they will only issue a licence for an increase in numbers if the planning for it has also been approved. The reason for the change is the proliferation of HMOs in the area that have put this on the political agenda for the local council leaders who insist that rigid controls are put in place.

So far, my local council has not gone to Article 4 planning enforcement that would prevent the establishment of any HMO without planning permission, but a much harder line is being taken and the two relevant departments have been brought into alignment on this matter.

An example of where personalities matter within a department that I can give you is regarding fire doors. I have several HMOs that were non-licensable only a few years ago simply because these were on two-floor levels only. At that time, I was told that a wooden door with intumescent strips and door closers fitted would be sufficient, rather than also fitting a more expensive thin 30mm fire door to fit the standard door jamb. Then after the change to licensing, for my HMOs with less than 5 people in occupation, I had to have these houses reassessed for licensing purposes.

The question was then about what they would say about my doors as the property now needed a licence. It could be that someone from the council may have just simply insisted that the doors needed changing, even though the assessed risk level had not changed. Because the person I deal with at the council on this matter is experienced in risks associated with HMOs, he took a view on this and, after consulting fire-safety LACORs guidance, he allowed me to continue with the same doors. It could have been different with a different council officer.

The statements above are of course very general and in relation to my experience with my local council. However, from what I hear from other landlords in other areas, it seems that this would be a generally accurate statement about dealing with most local councils.

Councils and Clean Ups

Councils will want you to clean up after your tenants to keep a property in good order, especially as far as its external appearance goes with any waste taking up residence in a garden or outhouse for example. This is both during a tenancy, if your tenants are not keeping things tidy and the matter gets reported, and after a tenancy when sometimes things are just left behind when they leave. The feedback you will usually get from the council is the mess is harbouring rats, as this adds a reason for urgency to their request.

At the end of a tenancy, I have tenants kindly let me know they have donated some furniture to me by leaving it inside the property. Some cheekily even ask for money for what is left behind. If it is an unfurnished let then the fact of the matter is I don't want any furniture. Quite the opposite, in that they need charging for leaving anything behind although with changes in lettings rules nowadays there is very little you can legally charge a tenant for!

No matter what, any mess is not addressed by the tenant will need to be addressed by you as the landlord. Whether this is during the tenancy or at the end of it. Usually, it is more pressing during a tenancy as the end of tenancy messes tend to just appear as they leave. This is where they decide what to take and what to leave behind for you to magically clear up for them.

The rub of this matter is you then have to get rid of the waste. Now technically speaking, this is classed as commercial waste by the council. This is despite them going to charge you council tax, if you are not already paying it. You are therefore paying for the service of using the local refuse centres (tips) but they are not allowing you to use those services. This may vary considerably from council to council.

This ridiculous situation is overcome if you live in the area and get a license to dump your own household waste at the recycling centres. It is not possible for them to know where the waste is coming from and it is household waste after all. If you are not living close by, the disposal of the waste becomes another cost as well as a hassle.

You will be restricted to how you can take the rubbish to a tip, whether or not it is classed as commercial waste and needs paying for or not. You will not want to use your car to put the rubbish in, although I have to admit to having done that for ease of dealing with things. If you do this, just be aware that black plastic bags do not always keep their contents inside! You can be left with a very bad smell for quite a while in your car if certain rotting processes allow liquids to escape and get out of the bagged up waste.

Much better is to take a trailer with the rubbish in it and keep your car in good order. There are however limits on sizes of trailers allowed by the council. Despite wanting to encourage recycling, the trailer sizes allowed only seem to go in one direction, getting smaller every so often. I had a good trailer that was not excessive in size and worked well for several years, now it is considered as too large and therefore I need a commercial license to use it for waste disposal.

Councils demand a lot from you but then don't facilitate you when you make the effort. This has been the name of the game for quite some years and getting more stringent as time goes by it seems.

Selective Licensing

Some local councils want to control landlords with their own made-up demands under an officially available scheme known as Selective Licensing (SL). This is where a local council believes they need additional powers to enforce control in areas that are often predominantly rented housing stock. As we have seen, controlling landlords is often viewed as an easy option for the council and so this is quite attractive to them to extend their powers over landlords.

The word 'selective' comes from the fact that they are supposed to start in the worst areas rather than apply these additional rules and regulations in a borough-wide manner. The areas that are chosen are supposed to be deprived areas that have the statistics in crime and other social matters to prove it.

The other word 'licensing' comes from the fact that they will charge each landlord to have a licence to rent out their property in that area which must then meet their particular SL housing standards. In addition to having to comply with what can be these local laws that are drafted by the local council at will, a landlord will also need to pay for the privilege of compliance; the fee is there to cover the costs of running the scheme.

This is an additional burden to a landlord and is probably due to the few rogue landlords who might have tenants who are driving up certain antisocial and crime figures in the area. The shame of it is that the councils already have considerable powers to deal with such landlords, including the power to shut down a property under certain circumstances.

As I have briefly covered before, the local council in my area was introducing this but we contested it in a two-year battle and finally defeated them in that they backed down from implementing it. We had to take it to a very experienced lawyer in the end, it was not an easy task. Should they have been successful in getting this passed, I am sure they would have spread it much wider, on the back of claims of improvements. I am pretty sure they would be able to show some improvements by using statistics. Let's call these 'selective' statistics!

In fact, in the areas they were proposing to implement SL, those areas were already showing improving trends even without the licensing imposed. No doubt the council would have claimed those improved figures would be as a result of their scheme. That is if it had been introduced in the original timescale before we started blocking it.

Just to give you an idea of how crazy things can get with SL, their proposal included a serious requirement to have all tenancies drafted in the language of the tenant taking up a tenancy. Not as though tenants follow what is written in the tenancy agreement anyway, no matter what language it is written in.

Other examples are that it would have included specifics on kitchen layouts that are above and beyond recommendations by national legislation for safety. This would come at a significant cost to any landlord needing to change the layout of their kitchen. These compliance costs would be far more than the licence cost, albeit just for complying with what we believed would give very little beneficial results.

Council Tax Exploitation

The empty property Council Tax policy is generally left up to each particular council based on general government guidelines. When I first started in property, it was commonplace that there was an exemption on an empty property for 6 months. This was a reasonable period to refurbish and let out a property without having to pay council tax as a landlord.

Then, at a certain time some years ago, that all stopped in our area, and landlords were then charged council tax from day one of having an empty property. In my investing area, there has now been a recent concession issued that gives me one month's grace period, but that is only if the property has been occupied for at least 6 months before becoming empty. However, this is still not enough time to fix up and let out a property again on the whole. We therefore end up paying council tax even though we are probably not using any of the councils' services.

If you are unlucky enough to have a property empty for a longer period, such as due to extreme tenant damage and not having the time or budget to deal with it, you may be charged double council tax as a 'long term empty' property. I get the reason for this as councils don't want properties to be empty, but it can be an added pressure when you are running a portfolio and you then run into this situation.

It can also happen when the council doesn't understand what you are doing such as when you try to explain you are doing short-term lets and therefore are paying the council tax yourself. I had this where I got charged double because they could not classify my property status on their standard system and it showed up as long term empty instead. I am currently contesting this.

If you are running HMOs then you will likely be paying the council tax for the house anyway. However, this is not enough for councils and they now see the chance to charge for each room, especially where there is a bathroom and food preparation facilities in a room. This looks like a new wave of landlord attack that is currently gaining momentum in many local councils.

Only students can get exemptions on HMO properties, but the issue is that you need the tenants to claim the exemption, or you will end up paying if they don't. However, they can't claim it in advance and you need to give them the tenancy agreement before they can claim. You are then having to chase them for it as the council comes to you for the council tax money rather than them.

Council Officer Incompetency

Don't be surprised when you are contacted by a local council housing officer over some matter. The initial contact might seem reasonable enough and if you simply do what they say all will be well and good. The problem is that some of them, in my experience most of them, will probably be doing what seems expedient to them and not necessarily effective overall.

It seems clear to me that they are measured by how many issues they resolve, and I use that word very lightly. In other words, they are measured by the number of cases they close with a satisfactory outcome as may be defined by their standards. This will determine how successful they appear to be and therefore affect their promotion prospects, hence future salary. Because of this, simply to get the case closed is the challenge at hand for them.

The most common matter to deal with will be a complaint to the council about you or a property you own as a landlord. In that case, it will just be a matter of getting action taken to the satisfaction of the complainant (they use that exact term actually when they write to you about someone complaining). If the person stops complaining then they have registered a success.

Because they are focussed on simply addressing the symptom (the complaint), rather than the root cause, this could cause you some inconvenience if you simply do what they say. One common thing will be to clean up an outside mess, such as waste not removed, created by a tenant. I object to this kind of instruction as it does not teach the tenant any lessons and actually reinforces their bad behaviour instead.

The shame of it is that the council have the ability to get the mess cleared up by council resources and then seek to claim the money back from the tenant, which would teach them a lesson. Because the council has more resources and professional and effective debt collection service, they will be able to impose this charge more easily than the landlord can. Irrespective, they don't go for that in my experience, but expect the landlord to clear it up and close the file on it to register as a success on their file.

This approach is quicker and less messy for them, yet the root cause goes unchallenged. Then of course the matter will return, even if you added the cost of the clean-up you had to do to the tenant's account. (Oh, I don't think you can do that anymore, as it is not a cost that is allowed by the latest legislation!). If you don't do what they say, they will use official powers to send you a letter to clear up the mess and you will have to do it. I don't clean up until that point.

I had one situation where I was asked to relocate some tenants because of some issues they had with alleged drug abuse and the neighbours were complaining. I resisted this for a long time as I could not have any of the complaints substantiated. For me, it should be a matter of taking action based on antisocial behaviour although the council simply wanted them moved in any way possible and as soon as possible. I told the council this would just be moving the problem and we would face the same issue again in a different location.

I made the mistake of doing what they said and relocated the tenants which cost me dearly in doing so (tidying up the mess at the old property, not getting their housing benefit payment for a while, and then seeing my new property degrade). Then, as you might guess, I got the problem again. You can guess what they are now asking me to do again.

In this way the problems are not dealt with, they are just dealing with symptoms and not root causes. This would be classed as highly incompetent management behaviour in my professional life in the manufacturing business, but the council seem to make it a way of daily management.

Another example of incompetency was when I was told I needed a structural engineer to calculate what I should do when simply removing stone cladding on a chimney breast when they assumed it was structural stonework. I went ahead and removed the cladding without contacting an engineer as it was clear they did not know what they were talking about (this was a buildings specialist as well!).

I don't want to go on listing examples of incompetency, but just want to make you aware that there will be numerous examples of this and you will have to learn to cope with it, as it can be very frustrating. They are evidently thrown into roles without much training and you will be part of their learning curve (although they probably won't want to listen to you if you try to explain what you think a better approach to a problem would be).

CHAPTER 7

Unexpected Costs

Tenant Damage

Tenants can severely damage your property and get away with it, leaving you with a bill far in excess of any deposit money taken. I can tell you now that tenant damage is a common problem. Taking a deposit will of course reduce this risk somewhat, although the government has made taking deposits about as hard as they possibly could, leading many landlords to wonder if it is worth the trouble of doing so.

In order to prove tenant damage and claim it against a deposit payment, you will need to have very well documented evidence of the condition of the property at the point of letting. This should come in the form of a photo or video inventory and written schedule of condition. Having these inventory reports done professionally and independently will be a good thing to do if you have a lot at risk with an expensive property, or one that is furnished very extensively with high-value items.

When you come to the end of a tenancy, you can survey the condition of the property and put any costs forward to the tenant for reasonable deduction to be made from the deposit paid. If they agree with you, all is well and good as they just electronically sign off what you have agreed. They will then get their residual amount and you as landlord get the amount to cover the damages.

In claiming damages however, you need to take into account the wear and tear of the goods, so you should claim a lesser amount than the cost of a replacement with a new item. This will not be considered if the tenant agrees with what you are saying, it only becomes an issue if there is a disagreement and the matter has to go to independent arbitration. In this case, the points of view and evidence by both parties is submitted for consideration and the decision is made independently against which you cannot appeal.

The time and resources taken to register and manage the deposit is quite considerable and, because of this, there has been a reduction in the number of landlords taking deposits. This, in general, is a bad thing as it means the tenant does not stand to lose anything should they damage something. This is of course excepting the minority of very genuine tenants who might even offer to replace something they have damaged. I have not encountered many such people, I am struggling to think of even one actually, although I am sure they exist, somewhere.

In the more extreme cases of damage, I would even call it criminal damage. This is where the damage appears to be deliberate and extreme. There would be no way a deposit can cover this extent of the damage. You might have some cover by insurance in this case, if you have a policy that includes such matters. There are even some buildings insurance policies that take this on and give you around £5,000 worth of cover for contents as well as the buildings cover. This would be for the fixed items at the property like the kitchen units and other fixtures and fittings.

In the case of such criminal damage happening, I have on some occasions contacted the police. I have done this in particular when this has been combined with the theft of items. If there is theft, it helps to have the serial number or other distinguishing markings recorded so that the police can go and retrieve the item from the tenant after leaving. However, this can be quite an onerous thing to do, to have to keep a record of the serial numbers, therefore theft is often difficult to prove if you don't have this information available. Damage is easier to prove, but still a challenge and little hope of a successful deposit claim challenge if you don't have an inventory signed off by the tenant.

Rental Houses as Drug Factories

A landlords' housing stock can make ideal drug factories for those growing marijuana. The cost of the rent compared to the value that a crop of marijuana makes it a deal-stacker for the growers. Stories of this abound and the drug trade in growing marijuana is quite considerable in the UK now, as you can probably tell with the pungent smell of it wherever you go. When you get a tenant who is growing a crop in one of your houses, the first you might hear about this is from a neighbour or someone who wants to split on them due to some personal dispute they have with them.

I have had both of these forms of being tipped off. With hindsight, I think I should have realised earlier simply because the tenants do not pose absolutely any problem, and if you ask anything of them then it is done straight away. This is very unusual behaviour for normal tenants, albeit exactly what we might dream all our tenants were like.

The rent is regularly paid, although if paid in cash by someone smelling of the plant, that will be a bit of a giveaway as well. Not that it is for sure this is happening, as many tenants are using cannabis now, that does not mean they are growing it.

If you made a visit to the property, you might not realise what is happening as the downstairs area is still used for the living area. This area might not be where your actual 'tenant' lives, but there will be someone living there to look after the house and the crop that is being produced. This in effect also becomes cover for what is really going on as people will get to know the occupant as their neighbour. Often, I have heard how pleasant these people are to the locals, and no wonder.

When you find out what is really going on, the police should be informed straight away and they can investigate. They will be happy to cooperate with you in this to 'bust' the house. Better that you go so you can open the door for them rather than them knocking the door down. Better still is to have the tenant there at the time, even if they are not expecting such a meeting with the police.

The police will only take action however if there is a crop being produced at the time. The one that we last 'busted' was full of equipment but no plants. The police quickly left without doing anything and said there was nothing they could do. You are then left with a house to put back in order and, as stated before, it could fall into the category of abandonment to deal with on top of that, if the tenant does not come back.

The damage you will face is the interference with the electrical circuits, various fastenings of equipment to the walls, holes in chimney breasts, and in ceilings to the roof space for the exhaust. This is not to mention the removal of all the 'kit' that they leave in there. This is said to have quite some value, but I am not in the market for selling that and just happy to dispose of it quickly.

There will be a lot of patching up of the walls to do and redecorating throughout. If your property was furnished when you let it, you will find that some of this furniture will have disappeared to make room for their equipment. Some of the more obliging such tenants have requested they have a furnished property offered unfurnished. I have gladly done this as if they were genuine tenants it would probably mean they would stay longer if they had their own furniture in there.

The amount of time to repair the damage can be considerable and the safety checks on the electrical system and reinstatement of the system will be required.

Police Enjoy Smashing Your Doors

The police have the right to put a hole in your rental property front door and then let you know you urgently need to come and fix it up quick, at your expense. This is in the case when they get a warrant from the court to do a raid on your house. This can be simply based on a rumour that something is happening at your property that is illegal. Even if they don't find anything and don't press any charges, you are still legally bound to pay the costs of the damage they have done in the process of drawing a blank.

To try to stop this, I have given my rental addresses to the local police with my phone number as the landlord. I can then supply them with a key if they have the warrant, or I can go and open the property up for them. However, this is rarely used (but has saved a few doors) because they prefer not to tell anyone that could leak something to the tenant, even though that will not be from me for sure. It is still worth giving them the details of your property addresses and your contact number if this can save you just one door, however.

I am not sure about exactly how many doors I have lost to raids, but maybe seven or eight over the 15 years I have been a landlord. The fix-up of the door can be problematic as the raid can take place at an inconvenient time when it might be hard to get your usual tradesmen to come out and attend. After they have broken the door for access, they just need it making secure before they can leave the scene.

If you can't attend quickly or get someone to attend, they will call out the tradesmen they use and that won't be at a good price, I can assure you. Add to that I have found the quality of the work of the contractors the police use is very poor in general. On one job the quality of work was so bad I refused to pay. The contractor even said it was done just to be good enough for 24 hours, but the price was triple of what a tradesman would normally charge for doing a good job.

I mean, how can you secure a property that is good just for 24 hours? It is either secure or not. I never paid. I was happy to go to court to defend their money claim against me that they repeatedly threatened me with. I ignored their escalating charges as they added extra costs for each letter sent to me. I also ignored their final offer to settle at a discounted price. Anyway, we digress.

The other problem to deal with is that they do not just take out the door alone, if it is a uPVC door, they will likely take out part of the frame as well because they aim the ram at the place where the frame meets the door. This makes it more difficult to fix up but normally some long screws will do the job where these are passed through the door panel and into the frame, or what is left of it. You can then repair the door properly later, which is likely to need a totally new door including the frame.

My issue with this is that the police can get away without paying for this. I know some have asked the police to pay and they have done so, but this is discretionary and I have always had to pay for the replacement of my doors. This is another thing you might find grossly unfair, but it is something you just have to accept as the cost of doing business in renting properties, especially high-yielding properties where there is more hassle for more money.

Court Action is Expensive

The court systems are expensive, even if you do the administration of a claim yourself. You might well have to resort to doing this yourself due to the costs involved in using solicitors, but it is still going to be expensive in terms of time, not to mention the ever-increasing court fees that will still need to be paid. All you can cut out of this is the cost of preparation of the court case application documents by the solicitor.

In taking the DIY route, you will have instead to invest your time in making sure you fill in the forms correctly, as one single mistake in filling in a form can lead to your case being thrown out of court on the day of the hearing. It is this level of attention to detail that you are paying for when you ask a solicitor to deal with it for you. Having said that, I have dealt with all my legal action on a DIY basis (mostly eviction proceedings for non-payment of rent, which is the most common reason).

It is now into double figures for the number of times I have been to court for this reason, yet so far only one case got thrown out. However, what I do now is take a solicitor with me on the day of the hearing and pay them for their expensive time for this. This is because they can deal more effectively with any questions that a judge can throw at you if they so wish. I don't want to risk all my time and effort in getting to that stage for the sake of a few more hundred pounds to pay a solicitor (it can cost much more, so shop around).

All this cost and time has led to the nonsense-sounding advice I have had advice lines give, which is to pay bad tenants to leave. This is in fact the last landlord advice I got for one particular situation, if you could successfully do with this with each bad payer it might not be a bad thing overall. It depends on your tenant, the less they earn (or are given) to live on, the more likely it is worth trying to pay them to leave. That would be less costly than paying to go through the court system and then have next to zero chance of claiming any rent owed later by way of the CCJ.

You have to think of the costs of the additional time which can be six weeks to three months before you get to court. Even after the court decision for them to leave, you have to see if they actually do leave and if not then you will have to pay for a bailiff to call to get them to leave. This can add additional time to the removal of the tenant, the actual time depends on how busy the bailiff is, but it could typically be up to six additional weeks or so.

There are other reasons that you could go to court, however, the one that I have experience on is for non-payment of rent only. However, I understand it is much harder to get tenants to leave based on other grounds such as antisocial behaviour, as the evidence has to be so compelling and not based merely on the opinions of neighbours. This kind of eviction proceeding would be less likely to succeed than simply claiming for non-payment of rent (which is easy to prove).

Irrespective, any action that goes through a court is going to be expensive in terms of the costs of time and money. As well as, in all likelihood, not getting the rent paid during the time awaiting the court hearing, as well as after the hearing as tenants usually get either 14 days or 28 days to leave. Then maybe even longer if hey still remain and you need to call the bailiff, which in my experience can take between three to six weeks, depending on how busy they are.

Agencies Won't Manage Like You

This is a very general statement, but one that is borne out in my experience. It is a fact that letting agents will not manage the property as well as you would. At least not with the same interest at heart is what I mean, and not in the administration sense which is what they should be good at to justify their fees. I have had a variety of agents manage my properties over the years but in the end, I have taken the properties back because I was not happy with their service in one way or another.

The longest relationship I had with an agent was, in fact, an agent that worked as a part of the local council, I was sure that they must be able to look after my properties better than I could. The council has inside information from the police that we don't have access to, and therefore any poor tenancies should be minimised I thought. I was wrong.

During my time with this agent, I was working abroad and gave the management of my properties entirely over to them for a period of around four or five years. When I took the properties back, I was shocked at the condition of them and each one needed pretty much a full refurbishment.

During the time they were managing the properties for me I was also sent quite a lot of bills for maintenance work done at each of my houses. These were not insignificant bills either, to put it mildly. Based on the level of the bills, I was fairly sure that things were being kept up on the maintenance side. In addition, the properties were being filled quickly enough so there was no cause for concern.

However, after about three years, the time taken to fill the properties was getting longer and longer. I was getting concerned. In addition, the rent payment record was getting worse and worse. It got to a point where I had to step in. When I did that I was shocked at the condition of the properties and realised there was no way I could get a decent tenant until a refurbishment was done at each property.

I confronted the agent about why the properties were so run down and the answer floored me; he said they were trying to save me money! Really? Not according to my bank account on maintenance costs. Not according to the length of the void periods. Not according to the poor payment record of the poor tenants that they were only able to sign up on my behalf.

All this is despite a weekly phone call for about one to two hours to get an update on what was happening, discussing what the issues were and actions that were going to be taken. This is the local council who manages the huge social housing stock they have as well as the properties of some private landlords like me. In fact, they have a small division of that company set up specifically to manage private rented sector properties.

In the end, I had no other option but to take the properties back and bring them under my management again when I returned to work in the UK again. Not that I wanted to do this, but I would otherwise be losing a lot of money month after month. I can tell you similar stories about other agencies that I have also had issues with. Maybe if you just have a few properties you might not come across this initially, but for a landlord with a considerably sized portfolio, you will find out what an agency is really like very quickly.

Therefore, don't just take it as read that the agent will manage your properties in the same manner as you would. Do you think they will feel as much pain as you when the rental income stops? Do you think they will be as keen to get you the best price for the maintenance work as you would? Do you think they will check on the quality of the maintenance work like you would, before paying for it?

Let me just end this section with a short story about an agent that is nationwide in operation and growing in size. They acquired a small agency that was renting out a property that is located remotely from me. At the time of the takeover, I recognised the respected lettings agency name and was very comfortable it would be well managed. I was wrong.

One day I got a phone call from the agent telling me that the extraction system was not working and the new tenant wanted it fixed as soon as possible. They had therefore called out an electrician to look at it and told me it needed the main fan unit replacing with a price of around £350 fitted. You can add VAT to that as well, like the companies they work with normally charge on top of the cost of the work.

I was a little shocked as this was a job and cost I was not expecting. As it happened, I was to be passing by the apartment on the way to Manchester Airport the following day. I therefore called in and checked it myself to see what the problem was. I had a quick look and soon found that the isolator was not switched on because maybe the previous tenant did not like the sound of the extraction fan whirring, and had turned it off.

Maybe that is enough said about how using letting agents can be an issue, and that it is not just a matter of handing them the keys and taking passive income, like we would all like to believe it is.

Who Let the Dogs Out?

Nearly all tenancy agreements I have seen say that a tenant needs to ask permission from the landlord to bring pets to live in the property. I have known tenants ask permission and, in all fairness, it is something that as a landlord we are supposed to agree to unless there is a good reason not to. Of course, landlords can ask for the property to be put back as though there had been no pet there when they leave. We can at least ask, getting what we ask for is often an entirely different matter.

However, there is usually a sudden breach of this condition without any communication whatsoever. By the time a landlord finds out about it, it will be too late and the dog smell is already there. This will probably take some getting rid of if it is quite pungent. It will likely need at least a change of soft furnishings and a paint of the property pretty much throughout. This should be the responsibility of the tenant to do this before they leave, but I would very much doubt that will happen in most cases.

Some dogs also like to eat woodwork, or scratch away at it. Low-level kitchen units are fair game for this activity as well as wooden doors and door frames. Dogs will also be put outside and may have kennels, which could be kindly donated to you upon the leaving of the tenant. That is if the condition of the kennel is that bad such as not be of value to the tenant or the dog(s) that is. Thanks!

The worst dog case I have had was during an eviction, which I touched on earlier, when there were seven dogs left in the house. Outside there were seven kennels built from breeze block. After getting the RSPCA to come and help remove the dogs and take them back to their owners (presumably) the clean-up of the mess could begin. The mess of the tenants was a fair competition to that caused by the dogs actually, close-call I would say for voting on a winner there.

If you really don't want dogs then you had better ask whether there are likely to be any they will be bringing to live at the property. There are some properties like flats where it would even be against the lease agreement to have a dog. In most cases however, it will be a matter of agreement with the landlord and ultimately at the discretion of the tenant whether one or more take up residence.

Legal Claims Against You

Legal cases can come against you for injuries you were nothing to do with. This was more prevalent when there was more legal aid available to low-income families. This is when the lawyers were advertising no win no fee deals for personal injury. I was lucky however to only have one case that went to court through this route.

Nevertheless, when you get such a case you will have quite some work to do. First of all, you will have to report it to your insurance company. They can then deal with the lawyer through whom the claim is coming. You will then be assigned to a solicitor to defend the case on your behalf which should be covered by your insurance, if you have good insurance cover that is.

You will need to help the solicitor to defend the case by sending them information requested, which will assume you have followed all the legal procedures correctly, as well as some best practices common in property lettings, but not a legal requirement. Record keeping is therefore important for the retrieval of this information, it helps if you are organised.

In addition to this, there will be requests from the claimant's solicitor for documentation that will try to erode your credibility by showing that you did not do everything you could have done, this will then strengthen the case against you. An example of this would be regular visits to check on the condition of the property. Good letting agents do this and it is good practice, but many private landlords will only be responding to breakdown matters reported by the tenant.

The claim I remember well was one not from a tenant, but from a tenant's sister, which I have touched on earlier. You are responsible for any injuries caused to others visiting your property, if the condition of your property is at fault. Anyway, the claim was for a broken wrist having fallen down the stairs due to a loose handrail, it was alleged. The strange thing here was that the tenant had left the property about a year before the claim was submitted. I had never heard of such an incident occurring, until the claim came through.

As the main defence for this, I could provide photographic evidence of an inventory that I made at the time the tenancy was taken out. This showed the property in good condition, and the tenant had not reported anything to the contrary in the time they had to respond to the inventory they signed. The claimant's solicitor said that I should have been visiting regularly to check all was safe at the property and made that the basis of their claim.

However, after I had supplied the inventory information, I never heard anything further and I never found out about the outcome of the case. I also never had any increase in my insurance premium because of this and so I assume the claim was not successful. Or maybe there was a small out of court settlement. Whatever the outcome, I was glad I had some good insurance in place as being a landlord owning the property in my own name, I was personally liable if the case was proven to be valid.

Actually, I don't believe for one moment the accident happened at my property by the way. As the case was brought to me by a no win no fee lawyer, in the days where legal aid was more widely available, I would expect she had fallen somewhere else and then decided to fabricate a story like that to make a claim. She would have probably been thinking that a landlord would be an easier target than who or what might have really been responsible. She could have been drunk and at her own home when it happened for all I know.

Irrespective, you will likely have to face some claims at some time in your property investing career. I hope these don't affect you when you are challenged by the claimant's solicitor, especially when you think the whole case is fabricated.

Tradesmens' Traps

Tradesmen are notorious for causing landlords difficulties. It is a love-hate relationship in most cases. We need to work with them to be effective, but more often than not there are issues with them not turning up when they should and having huge variations in prices for similar jobs.

A landlord needs to have a variety of tradespeople including joiners, electricians, and plumbers. Then there is the general small jobs person that we need which is often known as the handyman. These would normally be the most regular ones used on maintaining properties and refurbishing them when required. However, this can be the most variable in terms of cost and quality of all tradesmen.

With joiners, electricians, and plumbers you will have some degree of control as the jobs tend to be very defined and it is easy to get comparisons of quotations and also consider variations on the work that would do the job. With a handyman, it is much harder as the jobs tend to be more numerous and wide-ranging, especially on a light refurbishment job.

Looking at the work quotations for some handymen, I often think they must be on more per hour than a joiner, electrician, or plumber which are more skilled jobs where formal qualifications and continuing professional development certification are required. In addition to the high pricing for lower-skilled tasks, their trap is to get a price agreed on a job and then deliver something that was pretty much as described but not entirely as expected. Or the job quality is lower than would be satisfactory to the landlord. Next!

With all the trades (let's include handymen here too), the most common trap I have seen is increasing prices and a lowering of the quality of work. Sometimes these occur at the same time or sometimes separately. Clearly, the best prices and the best work is done when you first do business with them, but quietly things can change. I don't want to tar all with the same brush here, but just to say this is a trap I have experienced on a repeating basis over the years.

It is a real shame when things go this way because you then have to find another tradesperson to take on the work for you and you are going into the unknown again. Then the cycle continues. Lucky is the landlord who can maintain a stable and good relationship for many years, count your blessings. I have a few of these tradespeople who have been loyal to me for a long time and maintained fair prices at a good quality of work. Yet in other trades, I have had to change many times.

Maintenance Overload

The more properties you buy, the more maintenance demands seem to explode. Some properties can be left empty, even costing you money as you get on with other daily portfolio issues. As well as costing you a lot of money, these empty properties are also an insurance risk, as the cover is reduced for long term empty properties. I would say this started to happen to me when I got to around 20 properties.

Now I have 40 properties it can easily be that I have a few properties needing a good refurbishment in order to let them back out. Although I say just 40 properties, some are HMOs which means in total there is 100 units to manage, 100 tenancies to deal with. In that context maybe you can see how the odd one or two property repairs can easily get forgotten on the lengthy maintenance list.

This is not forgotten in the sense that we don't remember we need to do the work of course, but in the sense that we have to focus on other things that arise each day. You may be able to improve on this and be able to manage the workload better, in my case I have always found it a challenge to keep on top of things and keep everything in a state ready to let at any one time.

There will also be regular maintenance such as gas and electrical checks to organise. It is not just a matter of giving the addresses and contact details to your tradesmen, there is usually some co-ordination required to get them access to the house. Of course, with HMOs this is much easier as you can get them the key to the main door at least. Nevertheless, this is a challenge on top of the breakdown maintenance that needs addressing as well.

Another thing to account for is that tradesmen sometimes change their plans but don't bother to tell you. Therefore, you will be thinking that a job has been done only to find out a week later that it never got done. It is best to close the loop on each maintenance task and check at the end of the day how the task went. This does add even further to the administration work that needs to be done, but is really necessary to remain in control of your maintenance tasks.

Using electronic messaging communication makes this easier but still challenging. The more properties you have the more this will be an issue.

For really large landlords these are full-time positions and sometimes just one person is dealing with all maintenance matters where a landlord has several hundred properties to deal with.

If you get to this stage where you are losing control of existing maintenance, you might as well slowdown in your acquisition of new properties and keep on top of what you have. Your other alternative is to contract out the maintenance management work at a cost or employ people at another cost (as well as taking on the added responsibility of being an employer).

Apartment Management Fees

In England and Wales, there are management fees applied by a property management company for blocks of flats. This is not the same in Scotland, where costs for the common building are managed amongst the owners there without the need for a separate management company.

The costs for these separate management companies can be very high for what they do. You might think, well, what do they do? They are responsible to arrange common maintenance tasks such as looking after the apartment block grounds, repairs in car parks, as well as repairs to common parts of the building like the intercom, stairway carpets, lifts, and painting of common areas. On top of the costs for this work, of which most or all will be contracted out, they add a management fee of say 15% as a typical and reasonable figure. VAT will also be added to this.

These areas just given are the official ones at least. I was part of a group that took over the management of a block of flats and we had access to the books and we found various costs and missing receipts. This was from what is commonly recognised as a large and professional management company in the UK.

The behaviour in the details of the paperwork was far from what you would expect from the exterior of the company. It does not give me much confidence about the smaller management companies that are run by only a few people. However, maybe the smaller companies are more honourable than such high-profile property management companies. Certainly, I would not expect to see some expenses in there such as we found, like a helicopter flight over the city!

In any case, you will have to trust the management company you are paying, but this might simply be blind faith. All you get is a copy of the annual accounts, but not the details behind the numbers. There is a way to challenge the management company, however. If you can find enough owners, which needs to be in minimum of 50% of the owners in the block, it is possible to take over the management under a legal procedure known as Right to Manage.

This is maybe not what you are looking to get involved in when you are investing in property, but you just might have to get involved by default. I was not the leader of the group in our case taking over the management of the block, I was simply there to vote it in. However, as such a group member I got access to a lot of information in the process which did nothing to enhance my confidence in trusting those managing blocks of flats that are subject to management charges.

These costs of management charges are in fact something that can often turn a profit from an apartment investment in to a loss. These costs are not insignificant and can range typically from £1,000 per year to £3,000 per year, depending on location and what makes up part of the common areas of the main building. Seriously consider this before buying into what otherwise might sound like a good investment.

Note that you will pay these fees even when the flat is rented out. You therefore have to build in this cost element into the pricing of the apartment. However, the price of the apartment's rent is more set on what the market is willing to pay rather than the costs involved in providing the accommodation.

I can inform you that in some other parts of the world, the tenants will take on this charge during the time they are resident. This seems to make more sense to me as they are the ones benefiting from it. I have a flat in Budapest and it works exactly like that. I pay for the proportion of the block management charge when the flat is not rented, but the tenant pays it while they have the tenancy.

In our case however, in the UK, we are likely to see the payment by the landlord continue because there is security for the management company in getting paid. After all, a tenant can disappear at any time and might be difficult to chase for payment.

Ground Rent Shock

Another feature of apartment 'ownership' is there are ground rent charges that apply to each owner of an apartment in the block. This is a charge made by what is termed the Freeholder. This is the person or company that owns the plot of land that the building stands upon and there is a charge made on an annual basis for this.

It is common for ground rent charges to be issued every six months. These charges are paid directly to the freeholder who will issue a demand to you on a regular basis. These amounts at the start might seem fairly modest such as £150 per year, however, you will find in the lease agreement a schedule that shows the increase in the charge in future years which might very well give you a shock.

Due to the 'hidden' shock-cost that can come out to bite you like this, some freeholders will offer to sell the freehold claim to you so no further annual payments will be required. This in effect is paying for the ground rent in advance and getting a discount for doing so. Again, this will probably not have been a cost you were expecting to pay in the first instance, it becomes another cost that impacts on the profitability of your investment.

The best you can hope for is a ground rent charge that continues at a low rate for a long time and then increases modestly in the future. These are however the things you need to check at the outset because once you have signed the lease agreement then you are locked into that agreement and will need to pay.

If you do not pay, there are powers in the lease agreement for the freeholder to recover the money from you. In addition to charges being added for late payment or non-payment, the total amount can be added to any mortgage you have on the property and recovered from the lender, who will also add their administration fees for this. This can all be done without anyone going to court. I am aware of some people who have had this done to them when they simply could not afford to pay the fees from their own pockets. This was because the rent achieved was insufficient to cover these charges as well as their mortgage payments.

It is therefore not a light matter to consider, you will need to pay this charge come what may. For the reasons given above, some people simply avoid leasehold properties, amongst other reasons. Not least of which of these other reasons are the restrictions on what you can do in terms of modification to the layout of your apartment, which you will need to seek permission from the freeholder for.

Remote Property Maintenance Costs

You may get attracted to taking on a property deal that is a long way from where you live. Typically, this is defined as being more than an hour away as a visit would then be over two hours as a round trip, including what you went there to do. In these kinds of investments, it is easy for you to get ripped off by local agents for small jobs.

I have had some crazy prices for some small jobs even from nationally recognised letting agent names. You might also find that some of the maintenance companies quoting for the work have the same directors as the directors of the letting agent you are using. This can also be the case when you are using a nationally recognised letting agent name. Some of these agencies are simply franchises where people set up in business under such a recognised banner.

It would seem however that there is nothing to stop them from also setting up their own maintenance companies, which are definitely not operated at arm's length. These 'close' companies provide services to those local franchises rather than having a price direct from an independent contractor and charged at cost as part of the agency's maintenance service. The name of the company offering the maintenance work might offer you no clue whatsoever that there is any connection.

As a case in point, I had a quote of I think it was £180 + VAT to replace a faulty light switch and a shower hose. The job needed doing and it just happened that I would be passing by Nottingham, where the flat was located, on my way to the airport in just a few days' time (I travel a lot!). Therefore, I popped in on my way to the airport and did the jobs for less than £20 in materials costs. I think you can work out their extreme labour charges from there when the time in doing the work took me only 20 minutes at the most.

This is very nice work if you can get it, no wonder you might get maintenance quotes of this magnitude. Well let's face it, you are remote from the place so you are going to have to otherwise travel a long way to do it, if you don't happen to be passing by any time soon that is. Taking into account your time taken to travel and the trouble involved, I think there is a strong likelihood that you would just pay. Whereas if the job was local to you there would be no way you would settle for such obscenely high charges.

More recently, I had a quote coming through another agent for a problem with a washing machine at another remote property not working correctly. The quote given to me was £80 + VAT just to pay for a call out to see what the problem was, then on top of that would be parts and labour for doing the work. I refused this ridiculous price for effectively paying for a repair quotation and found someone on a google search locally who fixed it for £45 for labour only, and no VAT charge (it was just a twisted hose he said). I dread to think what the other contractor might have found and charged me for.

If you do buy into any remote property investments, it might be worth also investing some time in getting your own trusted maintenance people you can call on in that area.

Letting Agents That Add Margins to Maintenance

Some agents use other tradesman to do the jobs and then add their margins to the prices they are given. In my experience, I know this can be a 100% margin if they can get the basic services at a good rate, the charged rate to you then does not look too much out of kilter. If you had the time you could arrange this yourself for much less of course.

You might never find out who the original tradesman was as the quote you will see will be from a 'maintenance business' that simply arranged the work, or it might just appear as a maintenance charge on your monthly invoice and deducted from the rent. The letting agents I am currently using for my remote property investments supply me with the invoice as well as pay it for me from the rental income. That is unless I arrange the work direct of course, which they always give me the option to do. I often take them up on that option due to the ridiculous prices I would otherwise be charged, as discussed previously.

Of course, the main function of the letting agent is to find tenants and look after tenancies to keep the money coming in and keep the property in good order. You might well take a view on some of the infrequent higher charges for some maintenance work if you can get the stable income coming in. It is something to be aware of though and will be something you can either live with or not.

In any case, it presents an opportunity to save a little money but at the expense of a bit more work and inconvenience, or even getting your own hands dirty.

Education Expense Never Ends

If you are the type of person who just needs to keep up with the latest information and options you have in property investing, you can end up spending a small fortune for on-going education. I remember sitting through a three-day course over one weekend that cost about £3,000, and at the end of this they stated that to get the most from the information they shared, you should join their £18,000 mentorship programme!

I was sat next to someone and we debated whether it was going to be worth it. I remember him really struggling because he could see that at this price is about the same a deposit on an income-generating asset (a small high-yielding northern house). Regardless, he did go for the deal as the temptation of knowing what is on the other side was too much to bear. The fear of missing out is what gets most people to commit to such expense they would never normally consider.

The private educational systems in property investment always make sure there is a next step to take, to pay even more. This is not to say that some people don't get value from taking such steps and paying such money. In fact, the more you spend on something the more likely you are to value it. If you have spent a lot, you will be determined to get your money back in some way from the information you have paid for.

That is the way it has worked for me at least. I also know other investors where that is the case for them too. Some of these people I know were on the same property course with are now well-known on the property speaking circuit, and because of that get contacts to do more deals with. In that case, it is a win-win solution in that the property education providers make a lot of money from you. In turn, you make a lot of money from acting on their education provided as well as tapping into the network of people they attract.

You have to decide if you are an action-taker however and whether the spending of such money on property education is going to motivate you to take action. There is also the question of affordability and it should not be an amount that takes you into financial distress; you should never do that. However, an amount of money you can afford but which you would certainly want a return on, is about the right balance to set as a maximum to pay.

The crazy thing is that the information presented on the courses, of which I have attended a fair variety of in the UK, is nothing that is 'secret' as such. Attending such courses, assuming they are decent courses run by experienced people, will give you an action plan to follow immediately, however. Although the same information can be found in many sources on the internet and in books, it just takes time to distil it into a coherent and usable form to develop your own action plan. You are also out on your own rather than getting some support, which some property training programmes offer at an additional cost.

The fact remains, you can spend a small fortune on property education and the amount you are paying for a course today will only lead to a more expensive and tempting offer later.

Just make sure that whenever you pay for a course you are determined to develop an action plan to get a good return on your money invested. If you can't see you could do that with the information provided, then ask for your money back. Although don't always expect it will be given back to you, and expect the terms and conditions small print will be thrown at you instead, in most cases.

I think such courses should deliver on their promises and if they fall short you are within your rights to complain. Some courses offer you the option of leaving after the first half day for your money back, but again the fear of missing out will keep most people in the room. They know this of course, it is a proven formula.

Beware, Gazumping Still Exists

Gazumping is having an offer accepted on a property and then someone comes in with a higher offer and the seller decides to sell to them instead of you. Gazumping is not supposed to be possible, as when an agreement is made on a sale then the property it is taken off the market and no more viewings are allowed after an offer is accepted. This is only fair, as there are a lot of costs involved in arranging to make a purchase. To lose a deal halfway through will have cost you significantly both in terms of time and money.

It is therefore essential you get a memorandum of agreement on a sale before progressing with taking on conveyancing costs and putting in too much effort on the purchase of a property. Once I get the memorandum of sale from the agent, I am then comfortable that I can move forward without the risk of someone coming in with a higher bid and outbidding me. This memorandum will have gone not only to me but also to my solicitors and the seller's solicitors, who can then start work by issuing the purchase contract.

There is however one fairly common exception to this that has caught me out on a few occasions. In the process, it has also cost me a few thousand pounds and not to mention the wasted effort involved. You will do well to be fully aware of this situation so that you do not enter into it blindly and end up losing out too.

The situation that I refer to is when you are buying a repossessed property. You can of course get these at good prices as they want a quick sale. Despite wanting a quick sale, they also want to get the best possible price for the property and are willing to consider any new bids right up to exchange of contracts. To get to the exchange of contracts will however take time and money to do so.

The lender who has repossessed the property is doing this both in the interest of themselves to ensure they cover their costs, but primarily to be seen to be fair to the mortgagor who was repossessed. This is because the mortgagor (the ex-owner) will have to pay the bank any difference in what the loan amount and costs amounted to, compared to the amount of money received from the sale, after all costs. The mortgagee in possession (the lender) therefore keeps the right to continue marketing the property and the sales agent must show anyone around who expresses an interest in buying the property.

It is therefore best if you can buy these for cash and do it quickly, or at least get to the stage of exchanging contracts after which the sale is secure. In my case, I often had to purchase with a mortgage and therefore we needed a valuation and a mortgage offer to be made before we could even consider an exchange of contracts. There is then a good window of chance that you can get gazumped and end up out of pocket with nothing to show for it.

Garden Maintenance

Gardens should be maintained by the tenants and all you should have to do is provide them with the tools to do so. This is not the case with HMOs of course, in this situation you are required to maintain the common areas including the gardens. Even having provided the tools for garden maintenance you might find the tenants don't really have green fingers, to say the least.

You will then be faced with the problem of putting the garden back to something of a usable condition if you wish to let the property back out after the current tenant leaves. This is an additional task you will need to account for, not to mention any additional cost to pay for this in terms of either time or money or both.

What could be worse is that the garden is not used for the purpose it is meant for, but seems to be the second most useful application of the land. This is that it is used as a tipping ground. This can be for general waste or for larger items such as beds or sofas that are not wanted or exchanged for replacement ones inside the house. You can bet it is likely you will inherit this despite a tenant giving assurances that any mess will be cleared up soon.

Clearly, it is better to have low maintenance gardens to at least help with these matters. This comes at a cost if you have to convert the garden from a grass garden into something that will remain under control without much on-going attention. Buying a house with a traditional grassy garden therefore comes with some additional responsibilities and maintenance requirements.

Even where there is no abuse of a garden and even with some attempts to maintain, these will typically degrade over time and need a makeover when a certain time comes. You will know when that is when you come to market the property again and no matter what you have done internally, the outside area will let the property down.

Suffering from Tenant Fall Outs

I have had situations where a tenant has fallen out with someone, then that other person has taken it out on their house. Let us rephrase that, the other person takes it out on *my* house. These can be difficult situations where damage is occurring on a repeating basis. Your tenant might be going nowhere, and just reporting the matter to you for fixing.

Imagine that on an evening, the window of the house is broken with a brick in a hostile act by the party they have fallen out with. I can leave it to your imagination as to what the issue could be; there will be many possibilities and it is likely that you will never really know what the real situation is. However, you as the landlord have a duty to make the property secure and the costs will fall on you.

In my case, after having this a few times, I elected to board up the window and not replace the glass, because it was so expensive each time it had to be replaced. I figured that the property was secure with the boarding and that if I was to do any more securing work it would have to come to a point of getting reported to the council for me to take further repeated action. My pockets were simply not deep enough and it was costing more than the rent coming in on that property each month (not to mention there was a mortgage to pay each month).

In other cases, graffiti might appear with unpleasant messages on your property as a vindictive act against your tenant. You are effectively the innocent bystander who they won't care to even give a thought about. However, the council will come to you to clean it up, if the tenant doesn't do anything about it. Another act I have had a few times is paint thrown at the front of the house, which, when this is an oil-based paint, is very difficult to get off.

If you can get your tenant to admit any of this is something that they have brought to your property, you can of course ask them to pay for the costs. How likely do you think it is that this admission will be made and that the costs will be covered? In some cases, this has been successful for me, but in many other cases not.

These situations can be a form of great anxiety as you simply do not know how long this will go on for. There has always been the option in the past to request that a tenant leaves in order to bring this to a close. However, in recent times, you will probably be aware that the basis of such 'no-fault' evictions is being challenged and this might not be an option in the future. Where do you go with this kind of situation then?

There are no easy answers when you are a landlord suffering from tenant fallouts like this. Happy is the day when the tenant leaves, or the problems stop for some reason. These things probably don't stop because the tenant resolved the matter with the person that was doing the damage. Although you won't care about that of course, and again you will probably never find out the real reason it stopped. The offender going back in prison for some other offence is one such reason you might come across.

Tenant fall outs in HMOs can cause damage to your property from fights and attacks in the room a victim tenant is living in, or sometimes on the door or external walls to the room. I know of one landlord who has decided to make all his stud walls out of more expensive plywood rather than the normal plasterboard, this means these are very hard to damage. Clearly the occurrences of the situations described are a major part of the tenancy management in his portfolio.

You will probably just want the tenants to leave in this damage-prone situation, or at least the offending tenant. Again, you will be suffering the cost and inconvenience of the damage caused, as well as the loss of rental income. Keeping harmony in HMOs is not easy, and you are likely to suffer this way at some point. Albeit it is often not as severe and long-lived as the situation of single-lets described above.

Claiming Against Deposit Payments

We have touched on this before, where you are at a disadvantage when a deposit dispute arises. Ideally, any damage costs can be agreed between you and the tenant, and they simply get paid back any balance owing. However, they have a right to insist on independent arbitration if they don't agree.

As with most things in letting out property, it rests with the landlord to do the work on defending the case and supplying all the evidence. In general, although the arbitration is meant to be independent, there will be a bias towards protecting the tenant and you will have to prove what is claimed to be damaged, was actually damaged.

Having proved the damage done, and provided the costs of the items that need repair or replacement, you will then have to discount any value that would have been eroded from new by virtue of wear and tear. Therefore, it is not simply a matter that you can claim the full cost of the replacement, you must deduct a reasonable amount to reflect the reduction in value that will have occurred of the item being replaced. This is even though you are being forced to replace or repair the item simply because of tenant damage.

You can maybe now see why it is more likely you are to come to some compromise on deposit repayment with the departing tenant, rather than hold out for what you should be paid from the deposit ideally. This is because if you can bend somewhat to meet the tenant on the matter, you are going to avoid all this hassle in time and effort simply to get the full and proper value of deposit allowance paid to you. This is therefore another cost for you to absorb which you might not have planned for.

CHAPTER 8

Tenant Management

Performing Maintenance Miracles

You will be expected to perform maintenance miracles for tenants. Failure to conjure up the satisfying outcome of curing the problem as quickly as it takes to wave a wand may be immediately met with threats to stop rent payment. OK, that might be a little exaggeration, but only slightly.

The fact is there will be unrealistic expectations to dealing with maintenance problems. A landlord will have to deal with the tension between what tenants unrealistically will expect and what you are able to deliver, even with the best will in the world.

As already discussed, broken boilers can be one of the most common issues to deal with and these can be quite complex matters nowadays. Problems with boilers can be as simple as low water pressure that should be addressed by a tenant anyway, right up to temperamental problems on electronic printed circuit boards. To carry out some of the more complex problems may well require more than one visit by an engineer, but you will have seen to have failed in the eyes of the tenant if you don't get it sorted out quickly or get it done on the first attempt.

Other maintenance issues can relate to electrical circuits tripping out and taking other electrical services out with them. These can be tricky to sort out but often it can be the case of the tenant having plugged in a faulty appliance and the tripping out is in protection of that potentially causing a fire. However, the tenant will typically not want to hear that and instead will insist there is an electrical supply problem. In any case, if you can't go out and sort it out yourself simply by locating the faulty appliance or device, it is likely you will need to call an electrician.

It can however sometimes be a tricky electrical supply fault that is tripping out the circuits, this is especially so when using sensitive Residual Current Devices (or RCDs for short) to protect the circuits. Finding the source of such tripping can be very difficult, although rarely will a tenant be able to appreciate this and just want it fixing quickly.

Other problems that typically occur are leaking roofs or gutters, which can ironically only be safely fixed when it is dry. Therefore, this delay until it stops raining and dries out will not be appreciated and will simply be seen as a delay in getting the problem fixed.

I just give these examples above as the typical ones, although there are of course numerous other ones, such as radiators dropping off the wall and doors falling off hinges. Clearly, we know this does not normally happen unless there is some external force applied (read tenant damage), but it will still be your problem to get sorted out as soon as possible and often not fast enough to satisfy a tenant.

I think that is enough to communicate the general picture regarding maintenance issues and tenant expectations. On a positive, if you can perform in reasonably good time you will be seen as a very good landlord as the word gets around about other landlords who are not able to get anywhere near performing such miracles on maintenance. You therefore have a chance to stick out from the crowd if you can give a great response to maintenance issues, whether you are a miracle worker or not.

Tenants Lie

OK, that title is a little blunt and of course is not inclusive of all tenants. However, if you were to take what most tenants say to you as at the very least being exaggerated, if not a blatant lie, then you might not be far off the truth in most cases, in my experience.

I know renting to some foreign workers frequently sees them having to return home to their country because a parent has died. This was well before Coronavirus and the rate of mortality amongst tenant's parents is amazingly high. If you were to believe them that is. More likely they are trying to get a sympathy vote and tell a lie to get you to not pursue them for the final rent payments due and to try to get out of their contractual notice period obligation.

Another example lie you will get upon a tenant leaving your property at short notice is about a lack of maintenance or even damage to their health from breathing difficulties. This latter point will often be claimed to be due to damp they either did or did not mention to you during their tenancy.

Other lies by tenants are mentioned elsewhere such as those that relate to damages occurring for which they won't want to be held responsible for. Most common of which is radiators dropping off the wall and doors coming off the hinges in my experience.

Some lies can be a little less severe but equally frustrating, such as when there is a maintenance issue like leaking water that has not been mentioned until it is a real problem. In this case it could be that is has rotted the floor boards and cause problems with the joists, but they will say they have not been aware of it until they noticed the hole appear in the floor.

In all of these cases, it is hard to come out and say 'you are lying', and then say 'this is what has really happened... '. If you do then any remaining goodwill between you will be lost and you are likely to suffer some consequences in future. Typically, this could be by losing some money or some other form of loss like damage not being reported anymore and hidden until the tenancy is over.

The Abandoned Property Dilemma

As already touched upon, if your property is abandoned you can't just change the locks and re-let it out. Well you can if you want to risk being found on the wrong side of the law with a claim for illegal eviction. I know there are abandonment procedures you can take and that can minimise the chances and protect you if you are accused of this. But the fact remains that you are in a tricky situation if someone just ups sticks and leaves without saying anything (presumably they have stopped paying rent too).

I have heard the council talk about abandonment and treating it like there is a legal procedure to follow, and I have also heard the chairman of my local landlords' association comment on the correct procedures for it. But the fact remains that having followed all procedures recommended, there can be a claim made against you for illegal eviction. This can be brought against you either by the council or privately by the tenant. There is no legally valid abandonment procedure, just best practice to follow.

The only fully legal way to get your property back from the tenant is for them to surrender it to you. Leaving you the keys is enough. If they don't leave their keys for you, then you are in this situation of abandonment with a dilemma of what to do next.

If you ask for legal advice on this, it will be to put the tenant on a notice to quit. This will either be a Section 8 or Section 21 notice as appropriate, or at your choice if both apply. Then follow it up through the court papers and hearing, then finally call the bailiff if required. Only after following that long-winded and expensive route are you fully covered legally and can be absolutely clear of a claim against you for illegal eviction.

The alternative is to take a view on it and follow the abandonment procedures of asking around if anyone (such as housemates or neighbours) has seen them recently. If no contact can be made this way, you will need to put notification on the property, then later change the locks with a notice to contact you for access etc. Then finally taking the plunge and reletting the property out and taking the risk that they may return.

We had a tenant recently who we know has gone to the other end of the country based on his Facebook posts. However, they refused to communicate with us by any means and did not pay any rent for a long time now despite reminder letters, texts and phone calls which were all ignored. After a while we decided to clear out the property, which in fact was an HMO room. This room was starting to smell as so untidy and had organic matter rotting away (not a human body fortunately, or unfortunately, enough).

Lo and behold, it did not take too long before family members were saying they wanted the tenant's possessions which we had removed for safe keeping. They were saying that their relative had been evicted from his room and wanted his possessions. Good move by them to go on the offensive straight away and accuse of eviction rather than mention all the rent owing. These people are often specialists in renting and know more than you might like to think.

We nearly let the room out in fact because we were so convinced that he was not in the area and would not be returning. As it was, we could offer either room access for the tenant or surrender of tenancy, as well as return of the belongings. It often takes doing something like that just to bring a tenant to the table. At least they had belongings in there I suppose, it could be worse if they had nothing as they would have no reason to contact us, but they could still claim illegal eviction at a later date.

Hence the reason the legal advice lines will always tell you to go down the formal notice to quit route, how could they advise any other way? That is advised irrespective of this being almost prohibitively expensive and time consuming for the risk at hand. Therefore, the dilemma is with you regarding how you want to handle this. No easy solution, no risk-free option, except the long and expensive one mentioned above.

To finally put things in context, I can remind you about the approach of the local housing agency that is run by the council. After I gave them my properties to manage while I worked abroad some time ago, we had similar situations arise with tenants just leaving and owing rent, typically. When I asked them about what we should do, they explained they had an in-house lawyer but instead they invariably just took a view on whether the tenant had really left or not.

I have heard of very few cases of claims for illegal eviction. However, I have bumped into people from the council housing and welfare department taking such cases to court, when I have been there at the same time for an eviction case. Fingers crossed that I have not had one to deal with yet and have taken my chances on many an occasion let's say. Maybe one day it will catch up with me, but, on balance, any relevant fine will be less than the money I have saved by taking a view on this, as the council themselves did when managing my properties.

Even taking your chances is still an expensive exercise if you are going to follow the abandonment procedures, to try to justify yourself if the tenant suddenly reappears after a while. There will be those tenants who will have the cheek to contact you about you evicting them even though they might not have paid you any rent for six months or so.

Give and Take, Take, Take

I have found that the more you give tenants then the more they will expect. The more friendly you come across, the more they will feel comfortable asking for some things that are, well let's say, a little border line. At the end of the day you have a vested interest in them being happy and you may well want to satisfy them. Therein lies the trap.

It can vary from them wanting you to buy them a sandwich-maker in a furnished and fully equipped property, to new uPVC doors and windows and beyond. Don't be fooled into thinking that if you give them that it will be the end of it, they will come back for more later for sure. Better to manage this up front and quash their expectations, in the nicest possible way of course.

You will have to be the one that makes the judgement call on this but just be aware what else awaits if you too easily concede to them. At the same time, balance that with keeping good will between you in a landlord and tenant relationship. Remember they have possession of a very valuable asset of yours and you want them to want to look after it for you, but you can't be walked all over and meet their every whim either.

As with other things mentioned elsewhere, this is more easily handled if there is a letting agent between you and the tenant. I have found in this situation that the letting agent can manage expectations and take the emotion out of things. Even if you own the agency and it manages mostly your own properties, not many tenants will realise this and will tend to more easily accept a response from the 'agent' than they would from you as landlord direct.

Helping Vulnerable Tenants

Although we should all have our niche areas of investment and associated tenant types, it might be that your conscience calls on you to help the vulnerable in society who often don't have access to basic housing. This can be because of their personal circumstances or, as is often the case, an addiction or abuse of some kind leaving them in a desperate or even in a homeless situation.

It seems like a nice idea to have a business that can help others out and give back to society and try to help those who need it most. At some time in your property investing life you are likely to consider this. In fact, some do make it a central property investing strategy and do very well at it in terms of income generation. They create a successful business model whilst having a charitable aspect. Hats off to those who manage to do this.

Recent changes to the way housing benefit payments are made to tenants has made this area ultra-challenging. In the past it was simply a matter of choice for the tenant as to whether the rent was paid direct to the landlord or to the them before they passed it on to the landlord. Even those who are not in a vulnerable situation, and likely to be able to manage their income, would often elect to have the rent paid direct to the landlord. This would still help them avoid the temptation of spending it on other things and falling into rent arrears.

There are some exceptions where direct payments to landlords can still be made, but by and large you will still be looking to get the money paid on to you from the vulnerable tenant. Invariably it does not take long before they fall into arrears, then with data protection issues you cannot find out what is really happening and only have what little they tell you to go on. This can be hugely frustrating at times as you are unlikely to get the full and true story in my experience.

Add to this the fact that the bad habits they often seek to escape rarely results in long-term freedom for them from such vices. This is even after some have gone through established programmes of rehabilitation and then look for rehousing, with the assistance of the organisation that they have been working with. When the vices return the problems start again quickly and you have a time-consuming issue on your hands with the associated problems that are created, let alone the fact that loss of rent income often swiftly follows or even precedes it.

I am sure most of us would find helping such people really rewarding, but after quite a lot of years of trying with a part of my portfolio in this area, I am personally losing the strength to carry on in this area. You really need to have this area as a passion at heart I think, to be in it for the long term. The outcome of helping such people can sometimes be potentially financially damaging. You will therefore need some other kind of reward to be able to compensate for that, or it may easily wear you down.

Single Parents Rarely Come Single

When I first started in renting out single lets to the DSS market, the most common reasonable income-generating tenant type was a single parent. The current state of affairs mean that this is quite a rich market, at least in the sense of rich in choice. Most of my houses were two-bed terraced houses and ideal for such tenants.

In those days the rent was also paid direct to the landlord, for which most prospective tenants would be happy to agree to. The difficulty with these tenancies was not the person you have done the pre-tenancy checks on and their child(ren), instead it would be the person that moved in with them who is not even on the tenancy agreement. Theoretically, additional people have no right to live there, but you will have a difficult time enforcing this.

You therefore have a 'tenant of stealth' but one that will be happy to speak up on behalf of the tenant you signed up. They also have friends that they will be happy to bring to 'their' new house, and you will have to deal with the consequences of any antisocial matters this brings. Although these unofficial tenants are not always there for the long term, they can cause some issues while they are in situ.

Don't even expect you will get any money for the 'stealth tenant' taking up residence and causing extra demands on the tenancy. The way Housing Benefit payments work is that you only get paid per bedroom that the tenant household requires, therefore a single person needs one bedroom and so does a couple. The stealth tenant will also be claiming their benefits at your address without even having a tenancy agreement there; the council will not have any issue with this.

I always made it clear on the tenancy that no other person was allowed to use the property as their home under the agreement. This was specifically accepted but the fact remains that very many such tenancies ended up with a second adult resident that I was never introduced to beforehand. This can be another frustration and problem that might give you some cause for concern, but it comes with the territory and you will need to be aware of that.

Hoarder Horrors

You have a small risk of getting a hoarder as a tenant. For me it took over ten years before I had a hoarder. I had one in a house and I had two different people in separate HMO rooms in different houses. The first thought you might get is… who is going to be cleaning that up?! I mean it is disgusting, at least in the cases I was involved with. In fact, I have not heard of a tidy hoarder, it's a disorder that is hard to believe until you see it.

In one particular case, which I have to say gets my vote for being the worst (so far), nothing was disposed of and the room was full of waste. Take that to mean human waste as well! Bottled and bagged, as appropriate (note we are back in the 'sh1t' again here!). In addition, there were pizza boxes and take-away food containers galore; it was a fire hazard for the house. The tenant seemed nice enough to speak to and you would have had no idea of his disorder.

I got absolutely no sign of a problem. There had been an inspection on the HMO by the council about two years into his tenancy. I thought it was strange at the time when I knocked on his door and he would not open the door properly, with only his head visible at the door as we spoke about the up-coming visit.

At the time of the visit, the room looked to be in a normal condition. I can only assume it must have drastically worsened towards his leaving date. I use 'leaving date' lightly because he was always on time with his rent payment and after the last ever rent payment he made, he just told me he would be a little late with his next rent payment. It seems that was code for I am going to leave and never come back and I hope you can stomach cleaning up my mess I will be leaving you with.

It was hard to even open his room door on getting confirmation he had left. On entry, there were piles of waste in all kinds of containers and a bed and wardrobe visible somewhere in the middle of it. Luckily, at that time, I had the support of a local team who took the challenge on to clean it and restore it to former glory as a respectable HMO room. They had to get creative to safely manage the human excrement in bags and urine in bottles. The rest of the mess posed very little challenge in comparison.

Of course, all furnishings had to be changed and the flooring removed before disinfecting the room. Repainting to get the smell removed from the room helped too. This was quite a project and one you might be horrified to have to face by yourself. But someone would have had to sort it out. In the past, the person had to be me, as others had refused.

Fortunately, these events appear to be very rare, although there is the chance that you can get a hoarder and be left with their mess. I hope it is not as bad as my worst case, however in the other cases there had to be similar actions taken, despite not having to deal with so much 'human waste'.

Dealing with Tenants Direct

As already discussed before, face-to-face landlord-to-tenant contact is the worst and sudden requests for anything can throw you off your guard when you might be there to deal with something else.

Try not to get diverted on to anything that you did not go to see them about, and just say you will come on to their other matters later. Otherwise you will water down what you have gone to see them about (typically rent arrears) and just pick up another problem you did not have before you went to see them. Dealing with tenants direct is certainly tricky for a landlord, as we have touched upon before.

You might be the type that enjoys direct contact with tenants, that is a good thing if you have the time to deal with such matters. However, for the most part, I think property investors are normally focussed more on the property and enjoy that side of investing, rather than managing their tenants. However, you will not be able to totally isolate yourself from tenants if you rent out properties, but dealing with them direct is the very sharp end you might more likely come unstuck with.

There is also the meeting of potential tenants when you are doing viewings to letting out your property. At this stage, it is actually a useful thing I think to see who you will be letting to. You will be able to get a feeling for what the people are about and whether you are going to want to have them as your tenants. Ask them all the questions that come to mind and don't ignore what your gut tells you.

In this case, when you give this task to someone else to do, you are risking that they do a job for you that you will be happy with. It is a task that you delegate at your own risk. If you have a remote property investment, it is not likely that you can do the property viewings yourself. The same goes if you have a large property portfolio.

If you are just starting out in Property Investing however, it would be useful to get involved with tenants direct. In this way you can learn about tenants and how to select and then manage them to be good tenants for you. It will help you later in your investing career as you come to delegate this and may need to offer some support, although it will take up quite a lot of your time.

Ultimately, how much time you spend dealing directly with your tenants will depend on your nature as a person and what your objectives are with your property investing ventures. However, the main issues associated with this have just been presented for you to consider and decide if that is something you would like or not.

Obstructive Tenants

It can be very frustrating when you get obstructive tenants that can stop you doing what you need to do. Some seem to enjoy this, maybe because it gives them a sense of power that they don't normally have in most cases. Don't get me wrong, this is not that common, but when you get an obstructive tenant you will know about it. It is definitely the case that an Englishman's home is his castle (or woman for that matter).

This can range from finding it hard to make arrangements to simply getting the boiler serviced and checked, to installations of new equipment or even building fabric work getting stopped. You would think that anything that makes a property better for a tenant would be welcomed by them. Surprisingly, I have found that this is not always the case.

The reason for this could be that the tenants might not be intending on staying at the property for too long. In this case, the benefit they get compared to the disruption caused to them by an installation might not seem worth it for them. In recent times, I have been changing out the boilers in my houses and this has been the challenge to get these fitted with certain tenants.

Clearly there is a benefit to a tenant in terms of more efficient heating so in the main these have been welcomed by tenants. There have been some tenants however who have made the installation very difficult, even when the existing system is not operating correctly or efficiently. You simply cannot gauge people and be prepared that you will get some obstructive tenants, no matter what you are trying to do for them or the property they live in.

The big one that sticks in my mind is a planned installation of external insulation to a gable end wall. This in fact was to be done under European funding for the area and managed via the council. They were offering upgrades to local properties where this would be seen to benefit certain streets as a facelift and improve living conditions.

One property of mine qualified for insulation on the gable wall as it is an end-terraced house. The tenant was consulted and the work began outside. The roof was modified ready for the insulation that would effectively extend the wall outwards because of the fitting of the insulation. The scaffold was erected ready to fit the insulation. The final thing before fitting the insulation was that the boiler flue pipe needed extending as well.

This meant the engineers have need to go inside the property to fit that item. However, after all this work the tenant decided they were not going to allow the workmen in her house to do this work. They contacted me, I contacted her. However, she said she did not want them inside the house as it would make a mess during fitting, or similar such feeble excuse.

I was in America on holiday at the time and could not properly intervene and try to talk her around to letting it happen. By the time I got back from holiday, the council had taken the scaffold down and moved on to other jobs. I was left with a modified roof that needed attention to the soffits now, and therefore another cost to me rather than having an insulated gable free of charge.

We still get condensation and mould growth problems in winter on that wall, which would have been history if we had managed to get the wall externally insulated.

When You Wish Your Property Was Empty

No investor wants void periods where there is no rental income coming in. You have largely got all the costs to bare which have to be supported. The main cost is of course the cost of finance for most investors and this goes out of your account as regular as clockwork. A void period means you have to support the regular finance cost outgoings from other sources of income, be it other properties or even from any employment income.

When you have a void period, you will likely be doing all you can to get the property re-let. When the letting of the property is in place again you will feel some relief. You should have taken a month's rent in advance and you also have got a deposit paid as well. All well and good you will think and then you get on with other property matters or other things in your life.

There comes a time however when you may well wish the property was empty again. In fact, you may wish it had remained empty. This will be when you are getting problems with the tenant for bad behaviour or for not paying their rent on time, or not at all. These situations become a drain on you, either emotionally or financially, or both.

You will then regret the letting of the property and start to think it would have been better off if it had remained empty. At least if it was still empty you could do some work on it and improve its value or you could remodel it and make it worth significantly more maybe. However, with a problem tenant inside you cannot enter and you cannot easily make them pay you the rent they should be paying.

Sorting matters like this out takes a lot of time, not to mention the effort involved in finding solutions. This is why you will start to wish your property was still empty. This is a totally different viewpoint from the one you had when it was empty and you were wanting to fill it with a tenant as soon as you could.

I have a situation right now where I have just had a letter from the council giving me some ultimatums about the need to control the behaviour of the tenants. This was a property that was refurbished before they went in and even in the letter it states the condition of the property as being significantly degraded.

However, I remember at the time when it was empty really wanting to get a tenant in and could only see the rental income and getting it off my mind. We had gone through quite a significant repair and facelift exercise in the property. Not that we were making it a model example of that kind of rental house, but at least making it decent following a long tenancy that had just come to an end.

Now I am left thinking I wish it had been left empty. Even though I am getting the rent paid for it, the amount of work that will need to be done to repair it when I get it back forces me to regret filling it with the present tenants. Fortunately, this is an extreme case, and you might have much less severe cases. However, if you become a significant investor in rental property, I would be extremely surprised if you did not experience this feeling I describe.

Gimme My Wi-Fi, Water Can Wait

In some of the properties I rent out, I provide the Wi-Fi for the tenants. These properties are typically the houses in multiple occupation where each tenant has their own room in a common building. I provide this sometimes without having any other form of entertainment and they are quite happy with that. Televisions can be a hassle and it seems that most tenants use their laptop for such access to visual entertainment nowadays.

The thing that struck me most however is the utter panic when the Wi-Fi goes down for some reason. This can be because the supplier in the area is having problems or they are in the process of upgrading the network. You would expect there are other ways people can stay connected and entertained by the internet without having to totally rely on the Wi-Fi in the house. This seems not to be the case however.

I think there will be many times when the water supply is cut off when there are maintenance works being carried out on the street supply. In fact, I see some notices about this and about other water matters such as discolouration due to some system flushing that is taking place. In these water problem cases, I do not hear anything from the tenants; this is in stark contrast to when the Wi-Fi goes down.

Losing Wi-Fi for prolonged periods of time can cost you a lot of money as you will have very unhappy tenants. This is despite you not being able to do anything about it in most cases. There is the Wi-Fi technical helpline that you can call, although they will want you to be at the property if you are calling them for help, which can be a real pain if you are not in the area when the problem gets reported to you by the tenants.

The reason you will lose money is that tenants will not put up with prolonged Wi-Fi issues, especially when they are paying for it inclusive in the rent (even though it would only make up a small fraction of monthly property running costs). In this case they are likely to want to have a reduction in rent due to the inconvenience of it, or in some cases they will simply leave the property and go somewhere else to live. It is easy for them to simply go to another HMO room elsewhere, because they often don't have many possessions to take with them.

I have had this happen to me when there was a network with ongoing issues from a certain supplier (it always seems to be the same one!). I did try their helpline, but in the end, it was stated that it was that the network was overloaded in the area. As I recall, they gave me some discount on the Wi-Fi charges but that does not help much when you are suffering the loss of several room rents per month until it is fixed.

I remember this going on for several months and by the time the network was upgraded and working fine again, I had lost most of the tenants in that particular house. Thankfully it was only the one property that was so badly affected, despite me having other houses in multiple occupation in the nearby area.

There is nothing you can do about this, but just be aware how important the Wi-Fi is to the tenants and that they can do without water supply interruptions for longer than they can do without Wi-Fi. You will need to have some way of addressing matters as quickly as possible when any technical matters arise with the Wi-Fi, if you want things to keep on ticking over smoothly.

Letting to Students

Letting to Students has probably crossed the minds of most landlords at some point. With some landlords maybe having been students in halls of residence of shared houses, they will have had first-hand experience of this, albeit from the other side of the fence. I have been tempted with this lettings model as well, and in fact succumbed to the temptation.

The lure of letting to students was the calendar regularity of it in terms of arrival and departure times, as well as the fact that you do not have to pay council tax. (As mentioned before, the council tax exemption is only effective if the students apply for their exemption certificates, it is not automatic). It is also one type of tenant and therefore you would reasonably expect that all in the house will get on with each other.

Other attractions can be the typical parent guarantor-backed rent that you can get, so that if the student does not pay you have a responsible adult to reach out to for the money instead. As you can imagine, I had to do this on a few occasions and with no major drama, it has to be said.

On the downside, I think many will be aware of the reputation of students and parties. If you were a student at university, you might well have had first-hand experience of this, from the other side of the fence. The complaints from this will of course come from the neighbours, as did so from my first let to students on my very first night of letting to them. This can be short lived however, and then things settle down a bit.

I say a bit, because there will be repeats and other acts of irresponsible behaviour. The most serious of which I remember was one drunken student taking a 'pee' from a Velux attic bedroom window, by standing on a chair! Then he drunkenly lost balance and fell down the roof towards the ground for near certain death. Only having his life saved by falling onto a washing line which broke his fall before contacting the ground (this was a three storey drop). The first I heard about this incident started with the words… don't worry, he's alive!

He did live, but took about a year to recover from his injuries to get anywhere like back to normal life I heard. I did not hear back from him except for his parents to hand in his keys and end his tenancy term (they did pay me throughout the year actually). They also apparently did consider suing me, or so I heard, but decided that maybe there was a little too much input from their son on this matter for me to be held responsible. That would have been another claim my insurer would have had to get in involved with.

After such extremes of incidents, you have the common things to deal with like the end of the academic year. You would expect this to be a three-month maximum break. However, the universities and colleges tend to finish a month or two before the official end and tenants will be at you for wanting to end their tenancy early and not pay the last month or two's rent.

There is an answer for that of course, but it still makes for a pain to keep answering and trying to keep them on track with rent payments when they have already left. Associated with the same topic is getting the students to electronically process their deposit money back, after you have agreed they can have it back. This seems to be something they can't understand, in that they probably had given you cash and you had to transfer the payment electronically to the deposit protection scheme.

They don't teach how to get room deposits back on the courses they are on, and they can't seem to teach themselves. Even to 'google' how to do it is too much effort it seems, to get their money back. You can therefore get a lot of hassle about the return of their deposit money, because you can't just hand back cash to them, at least not if you use the custodial deposit scheme like I prefer to use.

That is just to give you a flavour for it. But it can also be very entertaining, if you like that kind of thing.

Household Splits

You may be renting to a family and everything is fine in that they came as a unit and passed all the referencing checks. Then at a certain point, the family or friendship inside the tenancy breaks down and you are then left with only part of the household you let your property to. This might be caused by a problem in terms of affordability or even someone new coming to live at the property that you had not carried out a reference on.

In theory, if the tenancy is drafted correctly, any new people coming to live at the house do not have a right to do so as they are not included on the tenancy. Some decent tenants might bring this to your attention and ask that you add them on to the tenancy document and you can do the checks at that point, before you do so. However, in most cases such people will just take up residency at the invitation of the remaining part of the originally occupying party, as we have previously covered.

If you find out about the change, you can raise the matter with the tenant with whom you have the original agreement with (the remaining part); but if they don't want to cooperate you will have a problem trying to enforce it. Your option could be of course to end the present tenancy and request the return of your property. This would however risk the relationship you have with the remaining tenant and that could lead to other problems.

I have had splits happen to the extreme where I am left with a person in the house that I have no agreement with and the original tenants have just left. This can be enforced more easily as the person has no right to be there and it could be considered a police matter. However, you then have the issue to know that the original tenant has really gone and you are not simply gaining possession of a property in an illegal way, which we have covered before.

The splitting up of tenants, and even splitting up of tenants with those they unilaterally invite to live with them, can become a problem to deal with. You might think that as long as the property is looked after and the rent is paid then all is well and good. That could well be the case, but you would need to know that the insurance is still in place on the property. This is because buildings insurances need you to have a rental agreement with the people living at the property.

The best thing you can probably do is get involved as soon as you find out about a situation arising like this. Have a discussion with those remaining and try to resolve together in a way that works for all concerned. It is when this communication fails that you have a problem.

A simple solution would be to write another tenancy agreement, after getting the departing tenant(s) from the original tenancy to surrender their tenancy by return of their keys and getting something in writing to confirm such. The tenancy agreement can then reflect the people living there after checking they pass the referencing requirements that you have for a tenant in that property.

If this happens all well and good, but think of the nightmare scenario that can happen if it does not turn out this way.

Deposit Registration is Very Onerous

Issues relating to claiming on deposits has been mentioned prior, but now I will go into some details about it and expand on the matter for clarity in terms of actually putting a deposit in place.

When I first started in property, not so long ago, the deposit amount was simply stated on the tenancy agreement and recorded as paid, with a receipt then issued. When a tenant came to leave a property, we would go and check the condition and if there were any problems, we could discuss an agreed amount to deduct from the deposit to cover any needed repair work. There were rarely any disagreements and often the deposit was returned in full, at least in my case as a landlord it was.

However, pressure groups claimed that tenants' deposits were unfairly being withheld by landlords. Whilst in reality, the situation was that many tenants would not pay the final month rent and claim that their deposit would cover that. Anyway, I suppose there would be some truth in what they say about some bad landlords and letting agents. The response to this however was for the government to introduce a hugely administration-rich approach to registering and protecting tenant deposits. If you simply look at the terms and conditions the tenants have to receive and accept, I think you see how ridiculous it really is.

Not only that, to make sure it was taken seriously, there was a penalty set of up to 3.5 times the deposit amount if the deposit is recorded incorrectly, or not at all. As if that is not enough, the law also provided that a landlord cannot even get their property back upon request if the deposit had not been recorded properly.

Some landlords decided to take the approach of increasing the amount of rent taken in advance, but that was addressed by the government putting a limit on this so that it could not be more than an approximate normal deposit amount of around a month in rent (5 weeks' in rent value being the maximum deposit amount). The truth is that even the deposit amount allowed is not enough to cover the damage that some tenants do and you will be left out of pocket quite easily, even if you still jump through the hoops to take the deposit payment in the first place.

In stark contrast, I have my property in Budapest where the agent there takes 3 months of rent as a value for the deposit payment. This has never been the norm in the UK as far as I know and just one or two months were common, even before the restrictions were brought in. As you might imagine, the apartment I have in Budapest is still in reasonable condition after 10 years of ownership. Where there has been some damage, a reasonable amount of money was held back to cover that.

Clearly you can see by this example that some countries have a bias to protect the landlord and their property, whereas the legal system in the UK has effectively total disregard to this in practice.

Administration Increases, Yet Tenant Fees are Banned

Increasing administration is the order of the day in residential lettings, but Administration Fees now banned and so you can't cover the associated costs easily. Some people say that this will just have to be built into the rent and that is true, as the costs will have to be covered in some way. However, there is a market rent that people see and beyond such a figure they might not even apply to rent your property.

Eventually market rents will have to adjust. In the meantime, the landlords will be absorbing these costs. This cannot continue and might lead to non-profitable outcomes for the landlord, although it might even lead to some deciding to exit the market in the short term. Finally, though, the rental income will have to adjust, at which point the government and media will simply point to greedy landlords putting up rents as usual. This is how it goes.

The Tenant Fees Ban did not hit the market as hard as it could have done however, as many landlords deal with their properties and management of them privately. They may not have been charging for the additional admin associated with such things as issuing How-to-Rent documents, carrying out Right-to-Rent checks, and administering Deposit Registrations. This is not to mention the comprehensive information pack that tenants need to acknowledge in order to protect your rights to have your property back later.

In the cases of letting agents, many employment positions were funded by the fees from tenants, therefore the agencies are now looking for other ways to cover such costs of administration, as well as reduce staff. I have just seen a new tenant check-out fee appear that I have never seen before. This is for a remote property I have where the tenant has just given notice. I am sure I will come across more additional landlord charges soon, that will be passed on to me to start to cover the deficit created. The rent will have to increase to cover these costs, I have just requested that increase on advertising (hoping the market can stand it).

With the admin fees now banned, there is still increasing administration to work on; such as the newly introduced electrical certificates every 5 years for any rental property. This is on top of the annual gas certification, annual PAT testing in some cases, and an EPC every 10 years. These are not all that onerous, but organising these must all be paid for from the rent now, rather than any charges associated with the tenants we need this certification for.

In the past, it would have been possible to cover the cost of one member of the rentals administration team for every 100 letting units or so using even just modest admin fees. Shame they simply did not cap these rather than put a ban on them altogether. However, Scotland had already gone this route so it was clear that England and Wales were sure to follow suit since the lettings industry stayed afloat in Scotland after implementation.

The sad thing about this is that this will all be in response by the government to stories and pleas from pressure groups previously mentioned. They were asking to ban the fees because some rogue letting agents and landlords were taking advantage of the system. The picture would have been painted that this was more widespread than it actually was and therefore needed general regulation (not true). However, as it now is, we have to deal with it and absorb the costs we could once cover by a simple and reasonable charge for services provided to tenants concerning finding them a place to rent.

What other businesses or industries face this kind of interference by the government I wonder? I can't think of any. How about let's ban vehicle MOT charges and have these done for free, let the garages absorb the costs? That won't happen and if it did, I think we know what would happen there for sure. Short and explosive rant over.

CHAPTER 9

False Investment Principles

The Passive Investment Myth

Passive Investment is a term that is used synonymously with property investing. You will hear this when people want to sell you information about property investment, usually at property course teaser-events. It is clearly a successful formula to use as I don't know any such training company that does not try to draw people in on this basis.

For sure there are elements of the property investment that you can consider as being passive, where no effort is put in but the money comes in. However, you will often be required to address tenant issues or look after the condition of the property in some ways which means there is *no way* it can be truly passive. I would say it is quite an active form of investment out of all the financial investment options that you have.

Mentioning this fact to people considering a property investment career could of course easily put them off. Far better to tell them something that makes this an invisible matter at that stage so they join up for the training course. An honest training outfit can then subtly break the news to them on the training course, although I don't remember many overtly doing that on the many courses I have attended over the years either.

Maybe they leave it until you reach their mentorship programme levels before they finally share the fact that property is very much an active investment activity. This is not to say it cannot be enjoyable, that is an entirely different matter, but to call it passive to me is potentially very misleading. If any property teacher has any real experience in property, they will know it is not passive, or their experience is far too limited for them to be teaching about property investment in the first place.

You can however farm out the more active work and give that to others to manage. If you do that, I would suggest you should be prepared to pay handsomely for that service and factor in into your deal calculations. Additionally, factor in that someone else will never look after your property as much as if you were managing it yourself, and there is an implied cost to that too.

To put it the perspective of my experience, out of the 40 properties I have invested in, there is only one that I bought and never went back to. That is the exception that proves the rule maybe. It is a remote property investment of mine that is managed locally and sometimes I even forget the exact address of the property, in terms of the specific door number at least. This means it is possible, but in my experience, you have a one in forty chance of achieving it, which are not good odds.

Property is NOT a Pension

It makes my blood boil when I hear people talking about a property as a pension. Some have even written books asserting such, books that direct you to attending their expensive training sessions on the topic of course. However, in property investment, there are no tax breaks that you would have with a true pension, quite the contrary. I remember having a heated 'discussion' on a well-known property forum with the author of just such a book, or rather one of his defending business partners I think it was; this was after I pointed out that it was fundamentally wrong to assert that property is a pension.

If we are to call a property portfolio a pension then we should say the same about any business. I worry about this comparison simply because it can trick people into thinking they are building a pension in property and then they totally miss out on the benefits of having a pension vehicle in place as well. I built up both, don't just rely on one of them.

The benefits of a pension from a tax point of view are too great to be ravaged by those who seek to replace a legitimate pension vehicle with a false equivalent. Not to mention the insult when this is solely to sell people books, training courses, and mentorships about running a property business. This is an outrage as far as I am concerned.

However, I do appreciate that property profits can form an income that can be used in your retirement years. Only that would be true, as I have said, of any good business that can be set up to run itself and generate a surplus of cash after covering all costs.

If you are going into property full-time, like the advocators of using a property as a pension might want to take you into, you will in fact have more of a problem with setting up a true pension. This is because when you are employed, the pension is generally set up for you with the employer's scheme and you don't have to do anything. You will be benefiting automatically from the tax breaks it brings; this is both in terms of breaks on income tax as well as breaks on taxation of pension scheme annual profits.

A proper pension discussion would be a book in its own right, and maybe a worthy one for property investors who can actually get a lot of synergy from pensions investments, if they make the right choices. That is a matter for discussion another day maybe. The point here is that you should not fall for the trap of just solely relying on your property business as future pension income and miss out on the benefits that a pension brings for saving, to truly fund your retirement years.

Property Prices DO NOT Double Every 10 Years

When I first started looking at property investment, the claim was not a doubling every 10 years, but every 7 years. Recently it seems to have gone back to a claim that property prices double roughly every 10 years (because they are not increasing very fast at all at the time of writing). A decade makes for easier thinking and, when property prices are not doubling nowadays at such rates, it makes for a nice claim to make over the long term. Of course, if prices were doubling quickly and faster than every 10 years then it would be more dramatic for the 7-year figure to be used; just as it used to be the last time there was rapid house price inflation.

Even at a doubling rate of every 10 years, it is still a very attractive idea. This might be statistically correct if you can go back far enough in history to make this true, although in recent times there has been a significant slowing of house price growth. Nevertheless, the claim of doubling prices every 10 years is a commonly used description of how property prices rise.

My experience during the time I have been investing is one more of stagnation in price increases. This is from the point of view of investing in the North of England. There are however pockets of areas, even in the North, where there has been appreciable house price growth. The thing is, you generally only find this out after the prices have increased so investment for capital growth is somewhat of a lottery in reality.

London has always been good for house price growth, which is well-known. It may also be susceptible to a crash if the fundamentals of supply and demand take a bit of a dive due to any big impact on the economy. The main issue with the house prices in London is the inability of rents to be able to support even the interest to be paid on any mortgages secured against the properties. Therefore, you will have to rely on capital appreciation to make the books balance, and that is somewhat of a gamble. Albeit a gamble that has been paying off handsomely for London investors for a long time now.

In my particular investment area, I have been hearing for a long time that the fundamentals are in place for growth in prices. There is an investment in new industries and warehouses providing increasing employment, there is also good development in general improvements in the area as far as the quality of life goes. Yet I have failed to see a significant change in prices over the last 15 years.

If I go back to the beginnings of my property investment activities, I remember seeing prices increase by about 15 to 20 percent over the first few years while I was investing. I therefore thought that the things I had been hearing must be true; this was an encouragement as I wanted to get a comfortable equity cushion behind me. Then came the financial crash of 2008 and prices fell by at least 20 percent, taking things back to where they were when I started, if not a little lower.

Be careful then if you are considering investing on the basis that the average is that prices of houses double every ten years. We always say investing should be for the long term, make the definition of long term much longer than ten years in that case. Maybe you are safer to look at 40 years or so to be on the safe side. After that amount of time you could expect a doubling of prices in any area, but don't count on it.

Armchair Property Investing

I don't know about you, but the idea of so-called armchair investing has always appealed to me. The picture I get in my mind is literally being sat in an armchair while my property investments are out there being managed and bringing in money. To make this a reality, there has to be someone doing the work. It is not likely that a property can look after itself, as you will have figured out by now.

Those that are doing the work for you will have to be very trustworthy and motivated to keep your property in good order and keeping it let out at a good rent. Where do you think you are likely to find these kinds of people? Don't you think they would rather be looking after their own properties than yours? Isn't this just sadly human nature to do that?

In that case, how can so-called armchair property investing really work? If you do want to do this kind of investing let me suggest that it should not be by investing in real estate. Sitting in an armchair is not the kind of place to be for getting the most from this kind of investment. I have known several property investors who have taken the armchair route and even been promised below market value opportunities, then handed over their investment pots to buy these properties.

The lucky ones, who did get a property for the money they paid, were not satisfied with what they got and preferred to offload it if they could. The promised capital gains and rental profits simply did not materialise and they were very angry with the person they put their trust in to deliver this service. This is especially because they had paid good money for such a service, in addition to paying for the deposits on the properties brought to them.

However, as stated before, once you have started investing in property, it is generally not so easy to exit in the short term without suffering some financial loss. Not to mention the other losses you might have suffered from emotionally and in other ways, such as time and costs of getting involved with the people who led you into this situation. I would like to be able to say it was different, but this is the common story I hear in property circles about experiences with 'armchair' investing.

I think the common term for it now in marketing is a 'done for you' service; maybe it should be abbreviated to a 'done you' service! It seems you will be gaining from your financial involvement and for none of the work needed to look after the properties. You can consider this one of the marketing appeals of such a 'done for you' service. It is well-known in marketing circles that you can charge the highest rates for this kind of service.

A common ploy is to get you to attend a training course where you are shown some of the practicalities of property management. You then at least have a resistance to getting directly involved because you see some of the work to do ahead of you in order to get to the status of being an active property investor. After that, you will be very open to the idea of someone doing all of that for you, at what seems like a reasonable cost at the time.

There will be claimed to be money in surplus at the end of all costs, and you are looking to make a long-term capital gain on owning the property as well. Because of this, it is very likely you would opt for the armchair option when it is offered to you. Money for nothing, and that is where the alarm bells should start ringing.

The problem comes when you leave the marketing people and make contact with the operational side of the organisation. This is when the costs turn out to be more than you expected, with the profits resultingly much less than you expected, if any at all. Let's not even think about losing money from such a deal, but I have known that happen too to some people.

CHAPTER 10

Miscellaneous

Your Drains Are Your Responsibility

Your local water authority no longer take responsibility for the drains that solely serve your property. Add to this that some drainage problems are larger than what a plumber can deal with. This leaves then a big problem for you to manage as not many of us are drain clearing experts like the local water authorities are.

There are some companies that can help and fill the gap between what a plumber can't do and what the water authorities will no longer help out with. It is as well to make contact with such companies in advance as you are going to most likely need them at some stage. Tenants tend to have a natural ability to block drains, whether that is from blocking the toilet with wipes and such like, or from trying to put down the sink what should really go in the bin (fat and mashed food for example).

Add to this the age of most properties that property investors invest in, this debris tends to get caught up in the gaps and joints of the old pot drainage pipes, some of which may have broken with ground subsidence or settlement. Making these drains function as originally designed could be a large job involving excavation and re-laying the pipes.

This is a quite a significant length to go to that is really unnecessary, all because the tenants discard the wrong waste down the pipes. I don't know any landlords re-laying drainage pipes and instead they have to persist with warnings to the tenants. However, educating tenants about the cause of the problem often done in vain, together with the costs of clearing the blockages, when these blockages occur because of this.

It would be much better if the water authorities could use their resources to clear the drains, for which they are still happy to charge us for in terms of drainage charges on our bills. I know it does not take much of their resources to do the clearing as they have high pressure water jets that do the job quickly and effectively. It seems such a waste of resource when they come out to investigate and then just leave saying it is a drainage problem on the landlords' side, and so they cannot help.

In fairness, if you ask them nicely to help you, they sometimes will. But it is up to the people attending the job. The reason they go out in the first case is more to do with making sure it is nothing to do with the general drainage system common to others as well, which would be their responsibility. It still seems to make no sense to me to not take responsibility for something that none of us really fully know what we have underground at our properties.

This seemed to simply change overnight from their responsibility to the property owner's responsibility. It was much better before, now we have another responsibility we could do without as landlords, due to the issues described above.

Shared Drainage Issues

Another cause for potential conflict is that drainage of neighbouring properties is sometimes shared. This can be shared at the point of the soil stack above the ground, or on the drainage pipes under the ground.

I had one neighbouring landlord contact me who was quite furious that a soil pipe from one of my properties went into his soil stack (the long vertical pipe). He was a landlord recently buying the property and seeing that this was the case he contacted me after getting my number from my tenant at that house. Upon checking the drainage plan, I could see that there was in fact only the one drain that was between the two properties.

It just so happened that the drain was more to his side of the joining part of the properties than on my side. As often happens with terraced houses, over the years the rear of the properties gets fenced off, as was the case in this situation. The fact that the drain we were sharing went underground on his side of the boundary was incidental (if you can call it a boundary, as it is really shown open access on the deeds).

I had to go back and let the landlord know this and that this is quite common on those types of houses at that age of property. This was a fact I learnt after speaking with the local water authority who advised me that this was the case. Not an ideal situation, especially if there is a blockage that comes back up the vertical pipe. Someone will have to sort that 'sh1t' out when that happens? How do you think that is going to go?

As you will have already found out, I have had foul drain blockages come all the way back up the soil stack, but not on a shared one yet. I think that delight still awaits me. Clearing these blockages is not easy, and can be quite messy, I can tell you much about that first hand but I won't go into it here and will spare you the thoughts. Those pipes are very heavy when full I can tell you, let's leave it at that and leave it to your imagination, which I doubt could fully conceive of what the reality of that situation is like.

Anyway, back to shared drains. As I said, these can also be shared under the ground and a blockage downstream will cause problems upstream. In this situation you might get their help, depending where blockage has occurred. Otherwise it will be down to you and your neighbour to resolve the matter using a private drainage company who, in my experience, are not cheap. However, when you are in this situation the money side of it seems not to matter as much, which is probably why their services are not cheap!

Dealing with Needles

A problem similar to getting a hoarder as a tenant, as far as getting the clean-up work done, is getting a property back where there has been a drug addict resident using needles. When needles are found during a clean-up by a contractor, the cost to remove the waste will blow up astronomically. Just one needle found and you will find that most cleaners will be running for the door, maybe rightly so.

However, as a landlord, you are left with the task of still having to clean up the place and prepare it for reletting. If you cannot find someone to do it safely at a reasonable cost, then it falls on you to do it and take the risk, which you can manage by putting in place the relevant precautions. Anti-puncture gloves and sharps disposal containers are necessary as well as disposing of the needles as special waste.

I have personally had to clear out a few of my houses in this way, often after I have been trying to help with housing and rehabilitating 'vulnerable' people, which has already been discussed. This does not mean it is exclusively a problem with such people, but that is where I have encountered it the most. One of the difficulties is that they hide the needles in places you might not expect, rather than use safe disposal containers after use.

Connected with this is the fact that you need to look very carefully for the needles as you have a duty of care to the next tenant. Having done all you can and reletting out the property there will be the stigma that the house was previously used in that way. You might be lucky if you don't have neighbours who are the type who like to keep the stigma alive by duly informing the new tenant upon first meeting them.

This stigma gives you another problem in terms of managing your relationship with your new tenant. However, it will get less with time, but the first let after the clean-up of needles, and the rest of the mess that often follows, is the most problematic to deal with.

When White Paint Turns Yellow

It is very disheartening to paint all the woodwork white only to find it turn to yellow very shortly afterwards. I have known two reasons for this, one is under your control and the other not (so much) under your control.

A fresh coat of white paint does wonders for the appeal of a property to gaining new tenants, a yellow look does the opposite and makes the property look very tired and unappealing, maybe even I would go as far as disgusting in the case of extreme yellow.

The first case I refer to is where it goes yellow is when you simply go and buy the cheapest white paint. I recall B&Q's own brand white gloss being one of the chief culprits for me. When you first look at the cost of white wood gloss or satin, I can see the reason you might be tempted to look for a cheaper brand. This is especially so if you are going to need three or four 2.5L tins of it. It could however be a very costly mistake in the long run, as you will be painting over it again before long. You might also lose some good prospective future tenants because of its turning to yellow.

When I say yellow, I do not literally mean a bold yellow colour, but it is more of a white colour with a strong tinge of yellow. That is enough to take the brightness of the fresh white colour appeal away from it, something you would have seen when you first applied it. It is a fresh look that makes the painting worthwhile, whether you painted it yourself or paid someone to paint it for you. However, it will only get more yellow in appearance with age and you will have no option but to paint it all again.

The other situation that gives you a strong yellow tinge in the white paint, is quite disgusting, at least it is to me anyway. This is when you have people in your property who smoke. It will be written into your agreement that no smoking is allowed inside the property, despite this you will get those tenants that chose to go ahead and smoke at will. Of course, they will have to forfeit any deposit to cover the costs of putting a smoky smelling room back to a fresh smell. But this will likely mean a full repaint and quite likely the disposal, or extreme cleaning, of any soft furnishings supplied.

The sad thing is that their deposit money will not go far enough to cover the costs of putting things right. There will also be the added time it will take to arrange and do the painting job. Where the smoking has been excessive, it will leave a yellow tint appearance from the deposits of nicotine on the walls as well as the woodwork. A full repaint will be required in all likelihood.

This kind of yellow is not only worse than the first kind of yellow discussed, this kind of yellow will take some covering up if it is heavily nicotine stained. You will need to put several coats on and might even need to use some stain blocker in places where stubborn stains will not move so easily. I have known some people wash the nicotine off where it is really bad, not a job that I would like to get involved with.

In fact, I did clean it off once, from a very badly stained ceiling, and never again. I think my preference would be to reskim the ceiling with plaster if I was every faced with that again.

Property Inspections

Be aware, if you are doing your own property inspections on your tenancies, you are very likely to be adding to your work list. Of course, you expect to pick up some maintenance tasks but you will also be confronted with at tenant who has had plenty of time to line up their wish list for you when you make the planned visit. You will then be put on the spot to say yes or no, or at least take the request on board to get back to them later about it.

You can of course flatly refuse but then you risk to upset your relationship with the tenant. The flipside of this is that you don't do any inspections on your tenanted properties, there is much more chance your property will get damaged or run down, which means a big turnaround costs when the tenant leaves. I backed away from doing the frequent property inspections that I was doing when I first started out, and for the reasons stated.

I wanted more time to focus on the new deals I was investing in and working on the details of the property refurbishments and alterations. The property inspections on top of that work was bringing too much unnecessary detail to the table that was taking my attention away from what I wanted to focus on. Then I got my just deserts when I started getting my properties back in a condition that was less than desirable let's say.

If you want to do inspections, I suggest you get someone else to do them for you rather than you as landlord going to do these. Ideally this would be a rental agent who manages the property for you. They can then cushion the blow, if you have to say no (I didn't meant that to rhyme, but at least you will remember it now!). There is also less chance that the tenants would ask for as many things as would happen if you were visiting to do the inspection.

If I have a rental agency involved, I definitely like to get the property inspection reports to check that all is well, and I don't get many silly requests coming through. This will be because of the two reasons I mention above which is they are less likely to ask and that if they do, the agent can shield me from those requests.

We have already discussed what kind of 'silly' requests you can get in the chapter about Tenant Management, so I won't go into such examples again here. Suffice to say however that a lot of small requests can build up into a large matter to deal with. Especially when there are other things that are competing for your time.

No Political Party to Support

We have to vote for someone in the elections, or rather we should vote for someone, but this is hard as a landlord as no political party seems to have your interests at heart. Landlords are relatively few in number and tenants are large in number; so for vote-winning, it makes sense for all political parties to appeal to the tenants rather than landlords.

I found it particularly hard to vote over the last decade. Without wanting to get political, I was brought up in a most solid Labourite family with a working-class background. To me, the Tories were toffee-nosed people who were not in touch with reality. Then when I got into the world of businesses, I changed my viewpoint and saw that we need business to be able to support jobs and for the economy to function efficiently. At that point, I switched and started to vote for the Conservatives in support of business and entrepreneurialism.

This seemed all well and good and they generally supported business as I had expected. Then all of a sudden, landlords suffered a massive overnight attack from George Osborne from the heart of the Tory Government. It was such an attack and at a level that I could not believe at first.

In fact, the taxation he brought in was so punitive it quickly became known as the anti-landlord tax, which we have previously covered. In short, it is a tax change that taxes landlords on fictitious profits (some appropriately call it a tax on business turnover rather than profit), meaning they won't have generated the money to fully pay for the tax inside their business. How could I continue to vote for a political party like this?

At one point, the best I could do was a protest vote, to vote Liberal Democrat but I guess even those would hammer landlords if they got into power. Therefore, no matter who is in power, expect that landlords will come in for a tenant vote-winning landlord-legislation hammering of some kind, or if not that, then a further tax-raising exercise. I still can't believe the tax legislation just mentioned got passed, but it did.

Either George Osborne can't add up, or he is extremely vindictive towards landlords. Some say that he had a bad landlord experience in his student days. If that is the case, he has made a lot of landlords pay for his revenge, or at least those landlords who own properties in their personal names, as so far property company ownership remains unaffected.

I don't ever see there being a landlord-friendly political party, until they socially need landlords more desperately to provide the housing that they can't. Landlords can in fact provide housing at a much lower cost than local councils can and often deliver it to a much higher standard, yet we remain vote-winning fodder for an attack as well as tax-raising targets for any political party.

Landlords' Blame

Landlords are an easy target for blame when things are not going right in the housing sector, as well as for some other social matters as well. This is used by the government, media and pressure groups. There will be general blame thrown the landlords way and often for matters taken out of context.

Whilst it is true there are some social ills that might be caused by the actions or inactions of landlords, the root cause is likely to be somewhere else, Landlords are used as a scapegoat for such matters that are otherwise hard to pin the blame upon. This in itself is not a problem for a landlord, as long as you are not the kind that easily takes offence at such naïve blaming tactics. The stories from the blaming game will often simply be accepted as being true by the public at large.

What will affect landlords, and cannot be ignored, is when landlords are targeted for such things as taxation which we have just discussed. These two things might seem like separate matters but in fact can be related quite closely. The reason for this is that a government does not want to make tax decisions that are unpopular. Therefore, if they can target landlords that have been seen to be the root cause of other problems, any increase in taxes is seen to be justified.

The same goes for regulation when more regulations come in and affect landlords, it is almost seen as a vote-winner to do so as it seems like the government are taking action against one of the sources of problems in society. The sad fact in all of this is that, despite the short term hit a landlord has to take, any additional associated costs will find their way down to the average renter in the street, who might well have thought it was a good thing to punish landlords this way. Even worse is the fact that a lot of new legislation comes in to force and creates this additional cost to society which is wholly unnecessary.

The Public Image of Landlords is Poor

As already mentioned, the public image of landlords is very poor, due to many of the factors already described and due to sensationalism in media stories. As a landlord, you belong to this band of publicly unpopular people.

The poor image we have as landlords is totally underserved on the whole. I don't see any improvement likely soon however, since it is based on a few truly rogue landlords that will not obey any of the new regulations that are brought in to try to control them. In fact, many councils already have the power to deal with rogue landlords but rarely use those powers to deal with them.

As a result, the actions of those rogue landlords get publicised and used to reinforce the generally poor image that landlords have. The general image is one that basically says landlords are rich people who use property to exploit those needing housing and don't care about the conditions they live in. This is hardly a fair description of the landlords I know, but it is the image that the pressure groups and media continually reinforce about us.

You might not mind what others think about you, which is the best way to be with things like this that you cannot control. Or you might be a sensitive person who would find this image hard to accept. In that case, this could be a source of major personal dissatisfaction for you in your respectable property investing activity.

Either way, it is something to be aware of and account for in how you publicly approach your investing, including what you say to other people about what you do.

CONCLUSION

We have looked at a wide range of 'toxic' issues associated with the practical side of property investment in the UK. Of course, some of this will apply to property investing in any part of the world; although I have dealt with matters peculiar to the UK in some detail, which is my experience. The information has been organised by each general topic area, which is reflected in each chapter title.

I hope this has given you some good insight into what to expect. If you are already into property investment, maybe there were a few 'heads-up' moments about future potential toxic issues as you read the lessons. This will help prepare you for matters such as you may not have encountered so far. As I have been investing for more than 15 years now, I will have experienced most of what you can expect will come at you at some stage of your investment career.

The objective of the book was to make you aware of many real factors that exist but which are seldom spoken about in other books, and definitely not covered very well, if at all, on most property training courses. Being armed with this information, you can now decide if property investment is really for you, or whether the potential challenges are going to be matters that will mean you are not best suited to this area of business.

Whilst we focussed on the negatives here, there are of course many positives. A decision to start or continue in UK property investment will be a matter of balancing up the positives and negatives. It is more likely that you are already aware of the positives of property investment than you would be the negatives. The positives are dished out freely in all areas of property investment promotional media, be it on the internet, in magazines, or at live property events.

Just in case you need to be reminded of what the positives are, I will be writing a book to cover those points as well. This will be aptly called *UK Property Investment: The Antidote!* In this book, I will additionally cover many of the points that are often touted as 'secrets' by those offering the property training courses. In fact, these are well-known facts to most property investors who have devoted themselves to the study of UK property investment and been involved in this area for some time.

You will do well to study that book shortly after studying this book, to get an overall balanced view of residential property investment in the UK. You will then be able to see if your feeling is still overall positive about property investment, or at least be aware of the pros and cons as you progress in this area. This will at least be a balanced view, which reflects reality more closely than would have otherwise been the case without this information.

Finally, if you do wish to continue in property investment, keep up to date with the changes in this area by involvement with others and by reading or otherwise educating yourself as you develop. The one area I spotted that was not well covered was that of financing buy-to-let properties, which was the reason I wrote the book *All About Buy-to-Let Mortgages* a few years ago. The information in that book is still current, I will update it with later editions when anything significant changes.

I recommend you study that book, in whatever format you choose (paperback, kindle, or audible), and then select your financing and your mortgage broker carefully in line with the information given in the book. Financing is the lifeblood of property investment and it can also have a great impact on your bottom-line profits. It is only worth making this effort however if you are still serious to go deep into property investment.

As you can see, I am generally trying to deliver information into this property space where there is a lack of details on such topics. I am happy to share my experience and my learning over the years so that you can do even better than I have. At my stage of investing, I feel mature enough to be able to write and pass this information on for your benefit.

I have additional information available from my website and additional support materials you can benefit from, both paid and free materials. By registering for either of these, will can also keep in touch and I can inform you when I have anything you may benefit from in the future.

For access to this further information and to keep in touch please visit my website www.buy-to-let-mortgages.org.uk and sign up as either a FREE or paid member.

I wish you all the luck and strength you need to be successful in UK property investment. You have my utmost respect as you continue in this challenging field of business. You deserve all the benefits you can get. In fact, I will now switch my attention to writing the sequel book that focusses on the benefits of property investing, now this book is complete. As already stated, the sequel book will have the very apt title of ***UK Property Investment: The Antidote!***

I hope to see you soon in the sequel book, or the book I wrote about most effectively using UK BTL Finance, to purchase property with 'no money left in', called ***All About Buy-to-Let Mortgages***.

Best Wishes.

Peter J How

P.S. I want to ask you a favour from you in giving this book a Review on Amazon, or any other platform from which you may have made the purchase. If you did not buy it from an internet platform, please leave me a review on Amazon in any case. This will encourage me to write more materials and hopefully from that I can assist you further in your property investing endeavours.

Printed in Great Britain
by Amazon